DOCUMENTATION GUIDE

to accompany

Anson / Schwegler

The Longman Handbook
for
Writers and Readers

Second Edition

and

Anson / Schwegler/Muth

The Longman Writer's Companion

Documentation Guide t/a The Longman Handbook for Writers and Readers,
and, *The Longman Writer's Companion*

Copyright © 2000 by Addison Wesley Longman, Inc.

Please visit our Website at: http://www.awlonline.com

ISBN: 0-321-06496-8

12345678910-DM-02010099

Preface

The Second Edition of the Documentation Guide to accompany *The Longman Handbook for Writers and Readers* and *The Longman Writer's Companion* is a conveniently sized, easy-to-use reference tool for students in the humanities or the sciences, as well as for those writing documented papers in all fields.

Derived largely from Part 6, "Using Citation Styles," in the Second Edition of *The Longman Handbook for Writers and Readers*, the *Documentation Guide* covers the four major documentation styles—MLA, APA, CBE, and CMS—all updated to show guidelines for citing electronic sources. In addition, the *Documentation Guide* includes a new chapter on Columbia Online Style (COS), developed by Janice R. Walker and Todd Taylor as a way to cite electronic sources in formats consistent with traditional humanities- and science-style documentation styles.

Each of the five chapters contains step-by-step instructions for using the documentation style, numerous model entries for various sources, and models for in-text citations or footnotes. In addition, Chapters 1 and 2 contain sample student papers showing MLA and APA styles.

Contents

USING CITATION STYLES

1

Documenting Sources: MLA

The MLA (Modern Language Association) documentation style offers you a convenient system for acknowledging your sources for ideas, information, and quotations and for directing readers to these sources. It consists of an in-text citation (generally in parentheses) and a list of works cited (presented at the end of the text).

USE MLA DOCUMENTATION STYLE IN . . .
ACADEMIC SETTINGS

When writing in humanities fields such as English and foreign
 languages
When writing for publications or groups requiring use of MLA style
When writing papers for an instructor who asks for a simple form of
 parenthetical documentation such as MLA style

CONSIDER USING MLA DOCUMENTATION STYLE (PERHAPS A MODIFIED FORM) IN . . .
WORK AND PUBLIC SETTINGS

When readers are not expecting a specific form of documentation
When you feel your subject and audience are best served by a simple,
 direct documentation style that seldom uses footnotes or endnotes
When other writers in the setting use either MLA style or a similar
 though informal system.

If the MLA documentation style does not meet your needs, consider
using these other documentation styles: APA (Chapter 2), CBE (Chapter 3), CMS (Chapter 4), or COS (Chapter 5).

For detailed treatments of the MLA documentation system, see the *MLA Handbook for Writers of Research Papers* (5th ed., New York: MLA, 1999) or the *MLA Style Manual and Guide to Scholarly Publishing* (2nd ed., New York: MLA, 1998).

1a Using in-text citations

The **MLA documentation style** uses a citation in the text (generally an author's name) to identify a source for readers. The citation helps readers locate the source in the list of works cited appearing at the end of the paper. Many in-text citations provide a page number to indicate exactly where in the source readers can find the particular information.

IN-TEXT CITATION

Although the average Haitian peasant calls himself a Catholic and views himself as such, he generally continues to call on his African ancestors' gods, or *loa,* for spiritual and emotional support. As one peasant put it, "One must be Catholic to serve the loa" (Metraux 59).

—FREDZA LÉGER, College Student

ENTRY IN THE LIST OF WORKS CITED

Metraux, Alfred. <u>Haiti: Black Peasants and</u>

<u>Their Religion</u>. London: Harrap, 1960.

Citations may appear within parentheses or as part of the discussion itself. They may refer to a work in general or to specific parts of a source (by including a page number).

Author's name inside parentheses. You can choose to provide the author's name in parentheses. For a quotation or for specific information, include the page number to indicate where the material appears in the source, as in *(Jenkins 134).* Do not place a comma between an author's name and a page number nor use *p.* or *pp.* to indicate page(s).

Comparing the writing styles of individual authors in classic Chinese literature is difficult because ancient China had "no concept of single authorship" (Liu 30).

Author's name as part of discussion. You can make the author's name (or other information as well) part of the discussion.

James Liu reminds us that it is difficult to compare the writing styles of individual authors in classic Chinese literature because ancient China had "no concept of single authorship" (30).

General reference. A **general reference** enables you to refer to the main ideas in a source or to information presented throughout the work, not in a single place. It may also refer to a book, an article, or some other source as a whole. You need not provide page numbers for a general reference.

PARENTHETICAL   Many species of animals have developed complex systems of communication (Bright).

The statement summarizes one of the work's main points, so the reference cites the work as a whole, not a specific page or pages.

AUTHOR NAMED
IN DISCUSSION   According to Michael Bright, many species of animals have developed complex systems of communication.

Specific reference. A **specific reference** enables you to document words, ideas, or facts appearing in a particular place in a source.

People have trouble recognizing sound patterns dolphins use to communicate. Dolphins can perceive clicking sounds "made up of 700 units of sound per second," yet "in the human ear the sounds would fuse together in our minds at 20–30 clicks per second" (Bright 52).

The page number gives the specific location of the quotation.

According to Michael Bright, dolphins recognize patterns consisting of seven hundred clicks each second, yet such patterns begin to blur for people at around twenty or thirty clicks each second (52).

The page number cites the specific source.

Writer's Tip

Punctuation and abbreviations are kept to a minimum when you use in-text parenthetical citations following the MLA documentation style. You do not place a comma between an author's name and a page number in a parenthetical reference, for example, nor do you use *p.* or *pp.* to indicate page(s), as in (*Jenkins 134*). (For advice on punctuating sentences containing parenthetical references, see p. 5.)

S T R A T E G Y

Use questions like these to help decide whether to make in-text citations general or specific and whether to make them parenthetical or part of the discussion.

- Am I trying to weave broad concepts into my own explanation or argument (general), or am I looking for precise ideas and details to support my conclusions (specific)?
- Will this part of my paper be clearer and more effective if I draw on the author's own words (specific) or if I merely point out that the author's text as a whole presents the concepts I am discussing (general)?
- Do I wish to highlight the source by naming the author (part of discussion), or to emphasize the information itself (parenthetical)?
- Will this passage be more concise, emphatic, or effective if I put the author's name in parentheses or if I work it into the discussion?
- Do I wish to refer to more than one source without distracting readers (parenthetical), or do the several sources I am citing need individual attention (part of discussion)?

Placement and Punctuation of Parenthetical Citations

In general, put parenthetical citations close to the quotation, information, paraphrase, or summary you are documenting. Place the parenthetical citation either at the end of a sentence (before the final punctuation) or at a natural pause in the sentence.

> Wayland Hand reports on a folk belief that going to sleep on a rug made of bearskin can relieve backache (183).

If the citation applies to only part of the sentence, put it after the borrowed material at the point least likely to disrupt the sentence.

> The folk belief that "sleeping on a bear rug will cure backache" (Hand 183) is yet another example of a kind of magic in which external objects produce results inside the body.

When you place an in-text parenthetical citation at the end of a long quotation set off as a block, leave a space after the ending punctuation, and then add the citation.

> Many athletes are superstitious, especially baseball players, but perhaps the most suspicious of all are pitchers.

> > On the days they are scheduled to appear, many pitchers avoid activities that they believe sap their strength and therefore detract from their effectiveness, or that they otherwise generally link with poor performance. Many pitchers avoid eating certain foods on their pitching days. Some pitchers refuse to walk

continued

Placement and Punctuation of Parenthetical Citations
(continued)

anywhere on the day of the game in the belief that every little exertion subtracts from their playing strength. One pitcher would never
put on his cap until the game started and would not wear it at all
on the days he did not pitch. (Gmelch 280)

If the material you are quoting contains quotation marks, use double
quotation marks to enclose the quotation as a whole and single quotation marks to enclose the interior quotation.

According to Dubisch, "Being a 'health food person' involves more
than simply changing one's diet or utilizing an alternative medical
system" (61).

1b Creating MLA in-text citations

In-text citations following MLA documentation style may take
slightly differing forms depending on the number of authors, the number
of volumes in a work, and the number of works being cited. (For advice
on placing in-text citations within a passage and providing appropriate
punctuation, see p. 5)

Guide to MLA Formats for In-Text Citations

1. **One Author**
2. **Two or Three Authors**
3. **Four or More Authors**
4. **Corporate or Group Author**
5. **No Author Given**
6. **More than One Work by the Same Author**
7. **Authors with the Same Last Name**
8. **Indirect Source**
9. **Multivolume Work**
10. **Literary Work**
11. **Bible**
12. **Two or More Sources in a Single Citation**
13. **Selection in an Anthology**
14. **Electronic or Other Nonprint Sources**

1. One Author

Provide the author's last name in parentheses, or make either the full name or last name alone part of the discussion.

PARENTHETICAL   During World War II, government posters often portrayed homemakers "as vital defenders of the nation's homes" (Honey 135).

AUTHOR NAMED IN DISCUSSION   According to Maureen Honey, government posters during World War II often portrayed homemakers "as vital defenders of the nation's homes" (135).

2. Two or Three Authors

Give the names of all the authors in parentheses or in the discussion.

PARENTHETICAL   A century ago, whale oil was used not only for lighting but also for making soap, wool cloth, paint, rope, and leather; the bone was used not just for corsets but for making umbrellas, furniture, springs, fishing rods, and luggage (Norman and Fraser 209).

If the book had three authors, the citation would read (Norman, Fraser, and Jenko 209).

AUTHOR NAMED IN TEXT   As Norman and Fraser point out, a century ago, whale oil was used not only for lighting but also for making soap, wool cloth, paint, rope, and leather; the bone was used not just for corsets but for making umbrellas, furniture, springs, fishing rods, and luggage (209).

3. Four or More Authors

Supply the first author's name and the phrase *et al.* (meaning "and others") within parentheses. To introduce the citation as part of the discussion, use a phrase like "Britton and his colleagues point out. . . ."

Much of the writing that schoolchildren are required to do takes the form of tests or teacher-designed exercises (Britton et al. 24).

If you give all the authors' names rather than *et al.* in the works cited list, then give all the names in the in-text citation (660).

4. Corporate or Group Author

If an organization or government agency is named as the author, use its name (shortened, if cumbersome) in the citation.

Even in 1969, critics of the government's anti-communist policies were challenging the government's decision to divert money earmarked for education, health, and other "more fruitful programs" into "so-called national security" (American Friends 118).

"American Friends" is the shortened name of the American Friends Service Committee.

5. No Author Given

When no author's name is given, use the title instead (in a shortened version if it is long). Begin the abbreviated title with the word used to alphabetize the work in the list of works cited.

On January 1, 1993, the former state of Czechoslovakia split into two new states, the Czech Republic and the Slovak Republic (*Baedeker's* 67).

The shortened title refers to *Baedeker's Czech/Slovak Republics,* a book for which no author is given.

6. More than One Work by the Same Author

When the list of works cited includes more than one work by the same author, add the title in shortened form to your citation.

The members of some Protestant groups in the Appalachian region view the "handling of serpents" during worship "as a supreme act of faith" (Daugherty, "Serpent-Handling" 232).

"Serpent-Handling" is a shortened version of "Serpent-Handling as Sacrament." In a parenthetical citation, add a comma between the author's name and the title.

7. Authors with the Same Last Name

When the authors of different sources have the same last name, identify the specific author by giving the first initial (or the full first name, if necessary).

Although a number of Hebrew texts mention rebellious demons under the leadership of "Satanail" or "Satan" (D. Russell 110), the story of Satan and the rebellious angels gets its fullest development in Greek sources (J. Russell 192).

8. Indirect Source

When your source provides you with a quotation (or paraphrase) taken from yet another source, you need to include the phrase *qtd. in* (for "quoted in") to indicate the original source.

The play combines parts of two others, Shakespeare's *Hamlet* and Samuel Beckett's *Waiting for Godot,* in a manner Harold Bloom describes as a "kind of interlacing between an old play and a new one" (qtd. in Meyer 106).

Meyer is the source of the quotation from Harold Bloom.

When referring to an indirect source, you should generally include in your discussion the name of the person from whom the quotation is taken. If the same information were presented in a parenthetical citation— (*Bloom, qtd. in Meyer* 106)—some readers might mistakenly look for Bloom rather than Meyer in the list of works cited.

9. Multivolume Work

Give the volume number followed by a colon and a space, then the page number: (*Franklin* 6: 434). When referring to the volume as a whole, use a comma after the author's name and add *vol.* before the volume number: (*Franklin, vol.* 6).

In the classic Chinese novel *The Story of the Stone,* the character Xi-chun outwardly accepts her fate but secretly wishes for a different life: "If only I had been born into a different family! If only I were free to become a nun!" (Cao 4: 177).

The author's name is Cao, the volume number is 4, and the page number is 177.

10. Literary Work

When you refer to a literary work, consider including information that will help readers find the passage you are citing in any of the different editions of the work. Begin by giving the page number of the particular edition followed by a semicolon; then add the appropriate chapter, part, or section numbers.

In *Huckleberry Finn,* Mark Twain ridicules the exaggerated histrionics of provincial actors through his portrayal of the King and the Duke as they rehearse Hamlet's famous soliloquy: "So [the duke] went to marching up and down, thinking, and frowning horrible every now and then; then he would hoist up his eyebrows; next he would squeeze his hand on his forehead and stagger back and kind of moan; next he would sigh, and next he'd let on to drop a tear" (178; ch. 21).

Note that there is a semicolon after the page number, followed by *ch.* (for "chapter"). If you also include a part number, use *pt.* followed by a comma and the chapter number, as in (*386; pt. 3, ch. 2*). For a play, note the act, scene, and line numbers, if needed, as in this reference to *Hamlet*: (Ham. *1.2.76*). For poems, give line numbers (*lines 55–57*) or, if there are part divisions, both part and line numbers (*4.220–23*).

11. Bible

MLA style uses a period between the chapter and verse numbers (*Mark 2.3-4*). For parenthetical citations, employ abbreviations for names of five or more letters, as in the case of Deuteronomy: (*Deut. 16.21-22*).

12. Two or More Sources in a Single Citation

When you use a parenthetical citation to refer to more than one source, separate the sources with a semicolon.

Differences in the ways people speak, especially differences in the ways men and women use language, can often be traced to who has power and who does not (Tannen 83-86; Tavris 297-301).

13. Selection in an Anthology

If your source is a reprint of an essay, poem, short story, or other work appearing in an anthology, cite the work's author (not the editor of the anthology), but refer to the page number(s) in the anthology.

Andrew Holleran concludes that the AIDS epidemic has led many people to realize that "the most profound difference between men may be that between the sick and the well, but compassionate people try to reach across the chasm and bridge it" (552).
The selection appears on page 552 of the anthology *Patterns of Exposition*.

14. Electronic or Other Nonprint Sources

Provide the name of the author, the title, or any other information readers need to find the appropriate entry in your list of works cited. You need not include a page number for electronic sources a single page long or without page numbering. For numbered paragraphs, give the number and use the abbreviation *par(s)*.

In contrast, the heroine's mother in the film *Clueless* died in an ironic and contemporary fashion: the victim of an accident during liposuction.

1c Informative footnotes and endnotes

At times you may wish to comment on the usefulness or reliability of a source, provide some additional background details, or discuss a specific point at length. You recognize, however, that doing so would disrupt the flow of the discussion and would be useful for only a few readers. Informative footnotes (or endnotes) offer a solution. Place a number (raised slightly above the line of the text) at a suitable point in your discussion. Then provide the note itself, labeled with a corresponding number at the bottom of a page (for a footnote) or at the end of the paper on a page titled "Notes," coming before the list of works cited (for an endnote.)

[1]Anyone still inclined to question the intricacy of video games and the conceptual challenges they pose might consider investigating the numerous publications devoted to strategies for games like *Riven*, *Myst*, and even the various versions of *Doom*.

1d Creating an MLA list of works cited

In an alphabetized list titled "Works Cited," placed on a new page that follows the last page of your paper or report, provide readers with detailed information about the sources you have cited in the text. To indicate all the works you consulted, even if you did not cite them all, you may provide a list titled "Works Consulted."

In your list of works cited, alphabetize the entries by the author's last name or by last and first names for authors with the same last name. If a source does not identify an author, alphabetize by the first word in the title (other than *A, An,* or *The*).

Guide to MLA Formats for a List of Works Cited

1. BOOKS AND WORKS TREATED AS BOOKS
1. One Author
2. Two or Three Authors
3. Four or More Authors
4. Corporate or Group Author
5. No Author Given
6. More than One Book by the Same Author
7. One or More Editors
8. Author and an Editor
9. Translator
10. Edition Other than the First
11. Reprinted Book
12. One or More Volumes of a Multivolume Work
13. Book in a Series
14. Book Published Before 1900
15. Book with a Publisher's Imprint
16. Anthology or Collection of Articles
17. Government Document
18. Title Within a Title

continued

Guide to MLA Formats for a List of Works Cited *(continued)*

19. Pamphlet
20. Published Dissertation
21. Unpublished Dissertation
22. Conference Proceedings

2. ARTICLES AND SELECTIONS FROM BOOKS

23. Article in Journal Paginated by Volume
24. Article in Journal Paginated by Issue
25. Article in Weekly Magazine
26. Article in Monthly Magazine
27. Unsigned Article in Magazine
28. Article in Newspaper
29. Editorial or Letter to the Editor
30. Interview—Published
31. Review
32. Article from Encyclopedia
33. Selection in Anthology or Chapter in Edited Book
34. More than One Selection from Anthology or Collection (Cross-Reference)
35. Preface, Foreword, Introduction, or Afterword
36. Letter—Published
37. Dissertation Abstract

3. FIELD RESOURCES AND OTHER PRINTED RESOURCES

38. Interview—Unpublished
39. Survey or Questionnaire
40. Observations
41. Letter or Memo—Unpublished
42. Performance
43. Lecture
44. Map or Chart
45. Cartoon
46. Advertisement

4. MEDIA AND ELECTRONIC RESOURCES

47. Film or Videotape
48. Television or Radio Program
49. Recording
50. Artwork
51. Database: CD-ROM, Diskette, or Magnetic Tape
52. Online Source from Computer Service
53. Online Book
54. Online Journal Article
55. Online Magazine Article
56. Online Newspaper Article
57. Scholarly Project or Reference Database
58. Online Posting to Discussion Group
59. Synchronous Communication
60. Other Electronic Sources
61. FTP, Telnet, or Gopher Site
62. Work in an Indeterminate Medium
63. Email

1 Books and works treated as books

MODEL FORMAT FOR BOOKS AND WORKS TREATED AS BOOKS

period + space   period + space   colon + space
↓   ↓   ↓

Author(s). <u>Title of Work</u>. Place of Publication:

     Publisher, Year Published.
↑   ↑   ↑
indent five spaces   comma + space   period

- **Author(s).** Give the author's last name first, followed by the name (spelled out unless the author uses initials), any middle or initial, and a period . Do not include titles like *M.D.* or *SJ*, but include other parts of a name, like *III* or *Jr.,* placing them at the end of the name preceded by a comma: *Valantasio, Louis, Jr.* (See Entries 2 and 3 on this page and p. 14 for sources with more than one author.)
- **Title of work.** Give the title of the work, including any subtitle. (Use a colon to introduce a subtitle unless the primary title ends with a question mark, dash, or exclamation point.) Capitalize the main words, and end with a period unless the title ends with some other mark of punctuation. Underline the title, but not the period.
- **Publication information.** After the title, provide the city where the work was published, followed by a colon and a single space. If not obvious, add the country (abbreviated, as in *Dover, Eng.*). If more than one place of publication appears in the work, use the first one in your citation. Then give the publisher's name (followed by a comma) and the date of publication (followed by a period). You may omit unnecessary words such as *Publisher, Inc.,* and *Co.* (For example, use just *McGraw,* not *McGraw-Hill, Inc.*) Substitute the letters *U* and *P* for the words *University* and *Press* where they appear in the publisher's name (for example, *U of Chicago P*). If any of the basic publication information is missing , use *n.p.* ("no place" or "no publisher") or *n.d.* ("no date").
- **Spacing.** Double-space all entries, and indent five spaces for the second and any additional lines in each entry. Leave spaces between each of the major elements in an entry (author's name, title of work, and publication information).

1. One Author

Twitchell, James B. <u>ADCULTusa: The Triumph of Advertising in American Culture</u>. New York: Columbia UP, 1996.

2. Two or Three Authors

Give the first author's name, starting with the last name, followed by the other names in regular order. Use commas to separate the names, and introduce the second of two names or the third name with *and*.

Kress, Gunther, and Theo van Leeuwen. <u>Reading Images: The Grammar of Graphic Design</u>. London: Routledge, 1996.

3. Four or More Authors

Use the first author's name and then the phrase *et al.* (meaning "and others"). You may choose to give all the names, but if you do, you must list them in any parenthetical citations (see p. 7).

> Bellah, Robert N., et al. <u>Habits of the Heart:</u>
>
> > <u>Individualism and Commitment in American</u>
> >
> > <u>Life</u>. Berkeley: U of California P, 1985.
>
> **All authors listed: Bellah, Robert N., Richard Madsen, William M. Sullivan, Ann Swidler, and Steven M. Tipton**

4. Corporate or Group Author

Treat the corporation, organization, or government agency as the author, alphabetizing by the first main word of the organization's name. If the organization is also the publisher, repeat its name again, abbreviated if appropriate.

> International City/County Management
>
> > Association. <u>The Municipal Year Book:</u>
> >
> > <u>1998</u>. Washington, DC: ICMA.

5. No Author Given

List the work alphabetically according to the first main word of its title.

> <u>Guide for Authors</u>. Oxford: Blackwell, 1985.

6. More than One Book by the Same Author

List multiple works by an author alphabetically by the first main word of the title. For the first entry, include the full name(s) of the author(s). For additional entries, use three hyphens in place of the name, followed by a period and a space, but only if the author or authors are *exactly* the same for each work. If the authorship differs in any way, include the name(s) in full.

> Tannen, Deborah. <u>That's Not What I Meant! How</u>
>
> > <u>Conversational Style Makes or Breaks Your</u>
> >
> > <u>Relations with Others</u>. New York: Morrow,
> >
> > 1986.
>
> ---. <u>The Argument Culture: Moving from Debate</u>
>
> > <u>to Dialogue</u>. New York: Random, 1998.

7. One or More Editors

Begin with the editor's name followed by a comma and the abbreviation *ed.* or *eds.*

Achebe, Chinua, and C. L. Innes, eds. <u>African</u>

    <u>Short Stories</u>. London: Heinemann, 1985.

8. Author and an Editor

Begin with either the author's or the editor's name depending on whether you are using the text itself or the editor's contributions.

Weber, Max. <u>The Theory of Social and Economic</u>

    <u>Organization</u>. Ed. Talcott Parsons. Trans.

    A. M. Henderson and Talcott Parsons. New

    York: Free, 1964.

9. Translator

Refer to the book by its author, not its translator, even though the English words are the translator's. Abbreviate the translator's title as *Trans.*

Baudrillard, Jean. <u>Cool Memories II: 1978-1990</u>.

    Trans. Chris Turner. Durham: Duke UP,

    1996.

10. Edition Other than the First

Give the edition number (*3rd ed.*) or description (*Rev. ed.* or *1998 ed.*, for example) after the title.

Cowie, Peter. <u>Coppola: A Biography</u>. Rev. ed.

    New York: DaCapo, 1994.

11. Reprinted Book

Supply the original publication date after the title. If pertinent, include the original publisher or place of publication. Then follow with the publication information from the work you are using.

Ondaatje, Michael. <u>The Collected Works of Billy</u>

    <u>the Kid</u>. 1970. Harmondsworth, Eng.:

    Penguin, 1984.

12. One or More Volumes of a Multivolume Work

Indicate the total number of volumes after the title (or after the editor's or translator's name).

> Tsao, Hsueh-chin. <u>The Story of the Stone</u>.
>
> Trans. David Hawkes. 5 vols.
>
> Harmondsworth, Eng. Penguin, 1983-86.

If you are citing a particular volume instead of the whole work or several volumes from the whole work, supply only the particular volume number and publication information. Indicate the total number of volumes at the end of the entry.

> Tsao, Hsueh-chin. <u>The Story of the Stone</u>. Trans.
>
> David Hawkes. Vol. 1. Harmondsworth, Eng.:
>
> Penguin, 1983. 5 vols.

13. Book in a Series

Give the series name and any item number after the title of the work. Use abbreviations for familiar words in the name of the series (such as *ser.* for *series*).

> Hess, Gary R. <u>Vietnam and the United States:</u>
>
> <u>Origins and Legacy of War</u>. International
>
> History Ser. 7. Boston: Twayne, 1990.

14. Book Published Before 1900

For books published before 1900, include the publisher's name only if it is relevant to your research. Use a comma rather than a colon after place of publication.

> Darwin, Charles. <u>Descent of Man and Selection</u>
>
> <u>in Relation to Sex</u>. New York, 1896.

15. Book with a Publisher's Imprint

For a book issued with a special imprint name, give the imprint name first, followed by a hyphen and the main publisher's name.

> Sikes, Gini. <u>8 Ball Chicks: A Year in the</u>
>
> <u>Violent World of Girl Gangs</u>. New York:
>
> Anchor-Doubleday, 1997.

16. Anthology or Collection of Articles

To refer to an anthology or a collection of scholarly articles as a whole, supply the editor's name first, followed by *ed.*, and then the title of the collection.

> Zipes, Jack, ed. <u>Don't Bet on the Prince:</u>
>
> <u>Contemporary Feminist Fairy Tales in North</u>
>
> <u>America and England</u>. New York: Methuen, 1986.

To cite a selection within an anthology or collection, see Entries 33 and 34 on pp. 22 and 23.

17. Government Document

Begin with the government or agency name(s) or the author, if any. Start with *United States* for a congressional document or a report from a federal agency; otherwise, begin with the name of the government and agency or the name of the independent agency. For congressional documents, write *Cong.* (for *Congress*), identify the branch (*Senate* or *House*), and give the number and session (for example, *101st Cong., 1st sess.*). Include the title of the specific document and the title of the book in which it is printed. Use *GPO* for *Government Printing Office*.

> United States. National Research Council
>
> Committee on Global Change. <u>Research</u>
>
> <u>Strategies for the U.S. Global Change</u>
>
> <u>Research Program</u>. Washington: National
>
> Academy, 1990.
>
> United States. Cong. Senate. Committee on
>
> Environmental and Public Works.
>
> Subcommittee on Environmental Protection.
>
> <u>Policy Options for Stabilizing Global</u>
>
> <u>Climate Hearing</u>. 101st Cong., 1st sess.
>
> Washington: GPO, 1989.

18. Title Within a Title

When a book title contains another work's title, do not underline the title of the second work. If the second title would normally be enclosed in quotation marks, add them and underline the entire title.

```
MacPherson, Pat. Reflecting on Jane Eyre.
    London: Routledge, 1989.
Golden, Catherine, ed. The Captive Imagination:
    A Casebook on "The Yellow Wallpaper." New
    York: Feminist, 1992.
```

19. Pamphlet

Use the same form for a pamphlet as for a book.

```
Vareika, William. John La Farge: An American
    Master (1835-1910). Newport: Gallery of
    American Art, 1989.
```

20. Published Dissertation

Treat a published doctoral dissertation as a book. Include the abbreviation *Diss.*, the school for which the dissertation was written, and the year the degree was awarded.

```
Said, Edward W. Joseph Conrad and the Fiction
    of Autobiography. Diss. Harvard U, 1964.
    Cambridge: Harvard UP, 1966.
```

21. Unpublished Dissertation

Use quotation marks for the title; include the abbreviation *Diss.*, the school for which the dissertation was written, and the date of the degree.

```
Anku, William Oscar. "Procedures in African
    Drumming: A Study of Akan/Ewe Traditions
    and African Drumming in Pittsburgh." Diss.
    U of Pittsburgh, 1988.
```

22. Conference Proceedings

Begin with the title unless an editor is named. Follow with details about the conference, including name and date.

```
Environmental Impacts and Solutions. Proc. of
    the International Conference on
    Residential Solid Fuels, 3-7 June 1981.
    Beaverton: Oregon Graduate Center, 1982.
```

2 Articles and selections from books

MODEL FORMAT FOR ARTICLES AND SELECTIONS

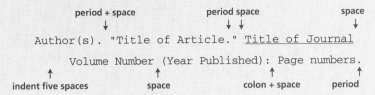

- **Author(s).** Give the author's last name first, followed by the first name, any initial, and a period. If the piece has more than one author, give subsequent names in regular order separated by commas with *and* preceding the final name.
- **Title of article.** Give the article's full title in quotation marks, concluding with a period unless the title ends with a question mark or an exclamation point.
- **Title of journal, periodical, or book.** Give the publication's title, underlined, but not including an opening *The, A,* or *An.* Do not end the title with a period.
- **Publication information.** Supply the volume number (and sometimes the issue number), the year of publication (in parentheses), and the page numbers for the full article or selection. The volume number is always found on the publication's cover or title page; even if it is in Roman numerals, use Arabic numerals for your entry. For a scholarly journal, you don't need to include the month or season (e.g. Winter). Introduce the page numbers with a colon.
- **Spacing.** Double-space all entries, and indent five spaces for the second and any additional lines in each entry. Leave a space between each of the major elements in an entry (author's name, article or selection title, and journal title along with publication information). Leave a space between the colon and the page number and also after the journal title and the volume number.

23. Article in Journal Paginated by Volume

Each volume consists of several issues, paginated continuously; that is, each issue begins where the preceding left off—at page 354, for example. Give the volume number after the journal's title.

Tobacyk, Jerome. "Superstitions and Beliefs
    About the Prediction of Future Events."
    Psychological Reports 68 (1991): 511-12.

24. Article in Journal Paginated by Issue

The issues making up a volume are paginated separately. Give the volume number first, followed by a period and the issue number.

```
Decker-Collins, Norma. "Freewriting, Personal
     Writing, and the At-Risk Reader." Journal
     of Reading 33.8 (1990): 654-55.
```

25. Article in Weekly Magazine

Put the day first, then the month (abbreviated except for May, June, and July), and then the year followed by a colon. Give inclusive page numbers. If the pages are not consecutive, give the first page with a plus sign (for example, 23+). (Treat biweekly magazines in a similar fashion.)

```
Wright, Robert. "The Power of Their Peers."
     Time 24 Aug. 1998: 67.
```

26. Article in Monthly Magazine

Treat a monthly or bimonthly magazine as a weekly magazine (Entry 25), but without listing the day.

```
Jacobson, Mark. "For Whom the Gong Tolls."
     Natural History Sept. 1997: 72+
```

27. Unsigned Article in Magazine

Begin with the title (ignoring *A*, *An*, and *The* when alphabetizing).

```
"Horseplay." New Yorker 5 Apr. 1993: 36-38.
```

28. Article in Newspaper

Treat a newspaper as a weekly magazine, including citation of pages (see Entry 25), but include the section number or letter with the page number. Omit *The*, *A*, or *An* at the beginning of a newspaper's name. For a local newspaper, give the city's name in brackets after the title unless the city is named in the title.

```
Pacelle, Mitchell. "When Blood Flowed Anew at
     Gettysburg, the Fur Flew, Too." Wall
     Street Journal 20 Aug. 1998: A1+.
```

29. Editorial or Letter to the Editor

Supply the title first for an unsigned editorial and the author's name first for a signed editorial. Identify with the word *editorial*.

> "A False Choice." Editorial. <u>Charlotte Observer</u>
>   16 Aug. 1998: 2C.

Use the word *letter* to identify a letter to the editor.

> Varley, Colin. Letter. <u>Archaeology</u> May-June
>   1993: 10.

30. Interview—Published

Treat the person interviewed, not the interviewer, as the author. For untitled interviews, include the word *Interview* (without underlining or quotation marks) in place of a title.

> Stewart, Martha. "I Do Have a Brain." By Kevin
>   Kelly. <u>Wired</u> Aug. 1998: 114.

31. Review

Give the title after the name of the reviewer. Cite an unsigned review by its title.

> Honig, Alice Sterling. "Helping Children
>   Problem-Solve." Rev. of <u>I Can Problem
>   Solve: An Interpersonal Cognitive Problem-
>   solving Program</u>, by Myrna Shure. <u>Day Care
>   and Early Education</u> 21.1 (1993): 34-35.

For a review with no title, give the name of the reviewer followed by *Rev. of* ("Review of"), the work's title, a comma, the word *by*, and the author of the work.

> Stuttaford, Genevieve. Rev. of <u>Imaginary
>   Homelands</u>, by Salman Rushdie. <u>Publishers
>   Weekly</u> 1 Mar. 1991: 61.

32. Article from Encyclopedia or Reference Volume

Begin with the author's name or with the article's title if no author is named. You need not include the publisher or place of publication for a common reference work or series; instead, note the edition and the date. If entries are arranged alphabetically, you need not note the volume or page(s).

```
Hansen, Klaus J. "Mormonism." The Encyclopedia
     of Religion. Ed. Mircea Eliade. 20 vols.
     New York: Macmillan, 1987.
"The History of Western Theatre." The New
     Encyclopaedia Britannica: Macropedia. 15th
     ed. 1987. Vol. 28.
```

33. Selection in Anthology or Chapter in Edited Book

List the author of the selection or chapter and give the title in quotation marks (but underline titles of novels, plays, and other works first published on their own). Next, provide the underlined title of the book containing the selection or chapter. If the collection has an editor, follow with the abbreviation *Ed.* and the name(s) of the editor(s) in regular order. Conclude with publication information and the selection's inclusive page numbers.

```
Atwood, Margaret. "Bluebeard's Egg."
     "Bluebeard's Egg" and Other Stories. New
     York: Fawcett-Random, 1987. 131-64.
```

If you are citing the original source for a selection reprinted in a collection, use the phrase *Rpt. in* ("Reprinted in") followed by information about the original source.

```
Atwood, Margaret. "Bluebeard's Egg."
     "Bluebeard's Egg" and Other Stories. New
     York: Fawcett-Random, 1987. 131-64. Rpt. in
     Don't Bet on the Prince: Contemporary
     Feminist Fairy Tales in North America and
     England. Ed. Jack Zipes. New York: Methuen,
     1986. 160-82.
```

34. More than One Selection from Anthology or Collection (Cross-Reference)

When you cite two or more works from an anthology or collection, include an entry for the collection and provide cross-references for individual selections.

Howard, Jean E., and Marion F. O'Connor, eds.

    <u>Shakespeare Reproduced: The Text in History</u>

    <u>and Ideology</u>. New York: Methuen, 1987.

Entry for collection.

Erickson, Peter. "The Order of the Garter, the

    Cult of Elizabeth, and Class-Gender

    Tension in <u>The Merry Wives of Windsor</u>."

    Howard and O'Connor 116-42.

Individual selection.

Goldberg, Jonathan. "Speculation: Macbeth and

    Source." Howard and O'Connor 242-64.

Individual selection.

35. Preface, Foreword, Introduction, or Afterword

Indicate whether the selection is a preface, foreword, introduction, or afterword. Give the title of the work and the name of its author, preceded by the word *By*.

Tomlin, Janice. Foreword. <u>The Complete Guide to</u>

    <u>Foreign Adoption</u>. By Barbara Brooke Bascom

    and Carole A. McKelvey. New York: Pocket,

    1997.

36. Letter—Published

Treat the letter writer as the author. Indicate the date or the collection number of the letter if the information is available.

Brevoort, Henry. "To Washington Irving." 9 July

    1828. Letter 124 of <u>Letters of Henry</u>

    <u>Brevoort to Washington Irving</u>. Ed. George

    S. Hellman. New York: Putnam, 1918.

37. Dissertation Abstract

For an abstract of a dissertation published in *Dissertation Abstracts International* (*DAI*) or *Dissertation Abstracts* (*DA*), follow the author's name and the title with the abbreviation *Diss.* (for "Dissertation"), the institution's name, and the date of the degree. Conclude with publication information for the particular volume of abstracts.

> Hawkins, Joanne Berning. "Horror Cinema and the
>   Avant-Garde." Diss. U of California,
>   Berkeley, 1993. <u>DAI</u> 55 (1995): 1712A.

3 Field resources and other printed resources

Use the following formats for sources other than books or articles.

38. Interview—Unpublished

Give the name of the person interviewed. Then indicate the type of interview: *Personal interview* (you did the interview in person), *Telephone interview* (you talked to the person over the telephone), or *Interview* (someone else conducted the interview, perhaps on a radio or television program). If a recorded or broadcast interview has a title, give it in place of the word *Interview*. Give the date of the interview or appropriate citation information for a broadcast or address (URL) for electronic source.

> Novak, Robert. Interview with Charlie Rose. <u>The</u>
>   <u>Charlie Rose Show</u>. PBS. WGBH, Boston. 29
>   Nov. 1993.
>
> Schutt, Robin. Personal interview. 7 Oct. 1998.

39. Survey or Questionnaire

MLA does not specify a form for these field resources. When citing your own field research, you may wish to use the following format.

> Arrigo-Nelson, Summer, and Jennifer Emily
>   Figliozzi. Questionnaire on Student
>   Alcohol Use and Parental Values.
>   University of Rhode Island, Kingston. 15-
>   20 Apr. 1998.

40. Observations

MLA does not specify a form for this type of field research. You may wish to use the following form to cite your notes on field observations.

```
Williams, Keyshawn. Observations of ATM
     Patrons. Aurora, CO. 11 Mar. 1998.
```

41. Letter or Memo—Unpublished

Give the author's name, a brief description (for example, *Letter to Jane Cote*), and the date of the document. For letters addressed to you, use the phrase *Letter to the author*; for letters between other people, give the name and location of any library holding the letter in its collection.

```
Hall, Donald. Letter to the author. 24 Jan. 1990.
```

42. Performance

Following the title of the play, opera, dance, or other performance, supply the name of the composer, director, writer, theater or place of presentation, and city where the performance took place as well as the date (include actors when relevant).

```
For Colored Girls Who Have Considered
     Suicide/When the Rainbow is Enuf. Ntozake
     Shange. Dir. Ntozake Shange. New Federal
     Theater, New York. 20 July 1995.
```

43. Lecture

Identify speaker, title or type of presentation, and details of the meeting, sponsoring group, location, date; include electronic address, if any.

```
Dunkelman, Martha. "Images of Salome in Italian
     Renaissance Art." The Renaissance Woman,
     II. Sixteenth Century Studies Conf., Adams
     Mark Hotel, St. Louis. 11 Dec. 1993.
```

44. Map or Chart

If the source is electronic, conclude with its address (URL).

```
Arkansas. Map. Comfort, TX: Gousha, 1996.
```

45. Cartoon

Provide the cartoonist's name and the title, if any. Include the word *Cartoon* and publication information (or electronic address).

```
Guisewite, Cathy. "Cathy." Cartoon. Providence
     Sunday Journal 23 July 1995: F3.
```

46. Advertisement

Begin with the name of the subject of the advertisement (product, company, or organization). Include the electronic address (URL), if any.

```
Ford Mustang. Advertisement. Elle Sept. 1998:
     158-59.
```

4 Media and electronic resources

47. Film or Videotape

Alphabetize according to the title of the work. The director's name is almost always necessary; names of actors, producers, writers, musicians, or others are needed only if they are important to identification or to your discussion. Include the distributor, the date, and other relevant information including the URL for electronic sources.

```
Rosencrantz and Guildenstern Are Dead. Dir. Tom
          Stoppard. Perf. Gary Oldman, Tim Roth, and
          Richard Dreyfuss. Cinecom Entertainment,
          1990.
```

For a videotape, filmstrip, or similar resource, indicate the medium—*videocassette, videodisc,* and so forth. If the date of the original version is important, add this just before the description of the medium.

```
Rosencrantz and Guildenstern Are Dead. Dir. Tom
          Stoppard. Perf. Gary Oldman, Tim Roth, and
          Richard Dreyfuss. Videocassette. Buena
          Vista Home Video, 1990.
```

48. Television or Radio Program

Begin with the episode title, and use it to alphabetize the entry. Give the program's name, and if they are pertinent to the discussion, include names for writer, director, actors, or others. Use abbreviations for their roles, for example, *Writ.*, *Dir.*, *Prod.*, *Perf.*, *Cond.*, *Introd.*, or *Narr.* Conclude with the URL for an electronic source, if appropriate.

> "Louie and the Nice Girl." <u>Taxi</u>. Dir. James
>
>   Burrows. ABC. 11 Sept. 1979.

49. Recording

You can begin the entry with the title of the recording or with the name of the person whose role in the recording you wish to emphasize, for example, the performer, the composer, the conductor, or the speaker. Underline the title of the compact disc, tape, or record. Put the name of a specific work in quotation marks unless the piece is identified by key, form, or number, such as *Symphony in A minor, no. 41.* Continue with performers or others involved, the manufacturer, and the year when the recording was issued. Indicate the medium if it is anything other than a compact disc (for example, *audiocassette,* or *LP* for a record).

> Short, Bobby. <u>Late Night at the Cafe Carlyle</u>.
>
>   Telarc, 1987.
>
> Mozart, Wolfgang Amadeus. Symphony no. 40 in G
>
>   minor. Vienna Philharmonic. Audiocassette.
>
>   Cond. Leonard Bernstein. Deutsche
>
>   Grammophon, 1984.

50. Artwork

Give the name of the artist, the title of the work, and the location of the work. Because many museum and gallery names are similar, indicate the city.

> Uccello, Paolo. <u>Saint George and the Dragon</u>.
>
>   National Gallery, London.

51. Database: CD-ROM, Diskette, or Magnetic Tape

Databases containing information or texts come in portable forms (such as CD-ROM) or online. Begin entries with author and title, provide publication information about the printed source (if any); give the title of the database or service (underlined), the medium (e.g., *CD-ROM, Online*), the name of the vendor or computer service, and the publication date (for CD-ROM) or date of access (for online sources).

```
Shakespeare, William. All's Well That Ends
     Well. William Shakespeare: The Complete
     Works on CD-ROM. CD-ROM. Abingdon, Eng.:
     Andromeda Interactive, 1994.
```

For abstracts, include information about an article being summarized, the electronic version, and any printed version of the abstract.

```
Blich, Baruch. "Pictorial Representation and Its
     Cognitive Status." Visual Arts Research 15
     (1989): 68-75. Abstract. PsycLIT. CD-ROM.
     SilverPlatter. 3 Mar. 1996.
```

52. Online Source from Computer Service

If you use a source from a service (such as Dialog, Nexis, or Lexis) and the source has been published in print as well as online, cite the source according to the appropriate model (that is, journal, newspaper, or abstract). Add information on the online version, including the name of the database (underlined), the word *Online*, the name of the computer service, and the date of access. Give the elctronic address (URL) or the keyword or topic labels (path) you use to reach it. If you used a service to which a library subscribes (such as EBSCOhost), give the name of the database (underlined), the name of the service, the library, and the date you accessed the source. If you know the electronic address (URL), give it at the end.

```
Blich, Baruch. "Pictorial Representation and
     Its Cognitive Status." Visual Arts
     Research 15 (1989): 68-75. Abstract.
     PsycINFO. Online. Dialog. 9 Sept. 1995.
```

The following models demonstrate the guidelines for citing electronic sources according to the 1999 *MLA Handbook for Writers of Research Papers*. The MLA recommends the following general conventions.

- **Publication dates.** For sources taken from the Internet, include the date the source was posted or last updated or revised; give also the date the source was accessed.

- **Uniform resource locator.** Include a full and accurate **URL** for any source taken from the Internet (with access-mode identifier—*http*, *ftp*, *gopher*, or *telnet*). Enclose the URL in angle brackets ⟨ ⟩. When a URL continues from one line to the next, break it only after a slash. Do not add a hyphen.
- **Page numbering.** Include page or paragraph numbers when given by the source.

53. Online Book

Include the author's name and the title; the name(s) of any editor, compiler, or translator (if relevant); electronic publication information (sponsoring organization and date of publication if the online text has not been published before); information about print publication (if any); date of access; the scholarly project containing the work (if any) and date posted (see following example); and URL.

> London, Jack. <u>The Iron Heel</u>. New York:
>
>   Macmillan, 1908. <u>The Jack London</u>
>
>   <u>Collection</u>. 16 Oct. 1996. Berkeley Digital
>
>   Library SunSITE. 1 May 1998 ⟨http://
>
>   sunsite.berkeley.edu/London/Writing/
>
>   IronHeel/⟩.

54. Online Journal Article

Give the author; the title of the article (if any); the name of the periodical; details about the volume, issue, and item number; and date of publication (in parentheses). If the number of pages or paragraphs is available, place a colon after the parentheses containing the date and give the number. Finally, give your access date and add the electronic address in angle brackets.

> Sheridan, Judith, and J. Devin McAuley. "Rhythm
>
>   as a Cognitive Skill: Temporal Processing
>
>   Deficits in Autism." <u>Noetica</u> 3.8(1998). 18
>
>   Dec. 1998 ⟨http://www.cs.indiana.edu/
>
>   Noetica/OpenForumIssue8/McAuley.html⟩.

55. Online Magazine Article

Supply the same information required for an online journal article.

```
Anderson, Christopher. "In Search of the
     Perfect Market" The Economist 14 Sept.
     1997. 5 Jan. 1998
     ⟨http://www.economist.com/
     editorial/freeforall/14-9-97/ec1.html⟩.
```

56. Online Newspaper Article

When citing an editorial, a review, or a letter to the editor, indicate it as you would a similar print source. See Entries 29 and 31 on p. 21 for examples. Otherwise supply the author's name, the title of the article, the name of the online version of the newspaper followed by the date of publication, and the date of access and electronic address.

```
Warren, Jennifer. "Assembly Bill Requires
     Parental OK for Body Piercing." Los
     Angeles Times 28 May 1998. 5 Aug. 1998
     ⟨http://www.aegis.com/aegis/news/lat/
     lt11997/lt970517.html⟩.
```

57. Scholarly Project or Reference Database

Begin with the title of the project or database and the name of its editor. (When citing specific material from the project, begin with the author and the title in quotation marks.) Follow with the name of the project or database. Include information such as version number, date of electronic publication or update, and name of any sponsoring institution. Conclude with date of access and electronic address.

```
"Imaging Radar." Ed. Robert Mah. Fact Sheets.
     Aug 1996. NASA Jet Propulsion Laboratory.
     3 Jan. 1999 ⟨http://www.jpl.nasa.gov/
     facts/⟩.
```

58. Online Posting to Discussion Group

Give the name of the author, the title of the posting as in the subject line, and follow it with the label *Online posting*. Next give the date of posting

and name of forum. Conclude with date of access and electronic add_
a forwarded posting, give the writer, title, and date of the document
phrase *Fwd. by* and the name of the person forwarding it, follow
phrase *Online posting,* the date of the posting, name of the forum, and _
tronic address.

> Harbison, Kimberly S. "Clic-liso Conference."
>
> Online posting. 5 Mar. 1999. The Discourse
>
> Studies List. 14 July 1999.
>
> ⟨DISCOURS@LINGUIST.LDC.UPENN.EDU⟩.

Many discussion groups maintain archives. For your reader's convenience, cite archived versions whenever possible.

> Wooly, Simon. "Re: Hooked on Ebonics?" Online
>
> posting. 24 Dec. 1996. Philadelphia
>
> Online: Talk Show. 2 June 1998
>
> ⟨http://interactive.phillynews.com/
>
> talk-show/schools postings/199.html⟩.

When citing a Usenet newsgroup, give the information on the author, title, the phrase *Online posting,* and date of posting. Give the date
of access. Next, in angle brackets, posting, give the name of the newsgroup, with the prefix *news.*

> Jarvilehto, Timo. "How Far Can Unity of the
>
> Organism-Environment System Be Maintained?"
>
> Online posting. 18 Dec. 1998. 19 Dec. 1998
>
> ⟨news: sci.journals.psycoloquy⟩.

Again, citing an archived posting from a newsgroup is preferable. In
that case, give the name of the group after the date of posting and follow
the access date with the electronic address.

> Jarvilehto, Timo. "How Far Can Unity of the
>
> Organism-Environment System Be Maintained?"
>
> Online posting. 18 Dec. 1998. PSYCOLOQUY.
>
> 18 Dec. 1998 ⟨http://x2.dejanews.com/
>
> =liszt/getdoc.xp?AN=424430517
>
> .1&CONTEXT=915464904.1241448542&hitnum=0⟩.

59. Synchronous Communication

When citing material from a MUD, a MOO, or another form of synchronous communication, begin with the speaker's name if you are citing only one. Give a description of the event, its date, its forum (e.g., *College-TownMOO*), and the date of access. End with the prefix *telnet://* and the electronic address in angle brackets.

```
Finch, Jeremy. Online debate "Can Proust Save

        Your Life?" 3 Apr. 1998. CollegeTownMOO. 3

        Apr. 1998 ⟨telnet://next.cs.bvc.edu.7777⟩.
```

For your readers' convenience, cite an archived version of material from a synchronous communication forum when possible. Provide the same information as above, but substitute the electronic address of the archived version for the electronic address of the forum at the end.

60. Other Electronic Sources

When citing electronic sources other than those explained above (such as a photo, work of art, film, or interview), adapt MLA models for their nonelectronic equivalents. Include the date of access and electronic address.

```
NASA/JPL. "Martian Meteorite." Photo. Views of

        the Solar System: Meteoroids and

        Meteorites. Ed. Calvin J. Hamilton. ⟨http://

        spaceart.com/solar/eng/meteor.htm#views⟩.
```

61. FTP, Telnet, or Gopher Site

For sources obtained through FTP (file transfer protocol), telnet, or gopher, supply information as you would for a similar source obtained via the World Wide Web, with the appropriate electronic address in angle brackets at the end.

```
Lewis, Deanna L., and Ron Chepesuik. "The

        International Trade in Toxic Waste: A

        Selected Bibliography." Electronic Green

        Journal 1.2 (1994). 29 Apr. 1996

        ⟨ftp://uiadaho.edupub/docs/pub/publications/

        EGJ⟩.
```

62. Work in an Indeterminate Medium

If the medium of your electronic source cannot be determined, give the description *Electronic* for the medium and list any information you can about its publication, the network, its sponsoring organization, and the date of access.

> "Red Scare." <u>Almanac of United States History</u>.
>
> Vers. 2.0. 1997. Electronic. Mount
>
> Pleasant Public Library, NY. 18 Dec. 1998.

63. Email

Begin with the writer's name and the title of the communication (in quotation marks), a description of the message including recipient, and the date.

> Smithee, Alan. "The Director Confesses."
>
> E-mail to the author. 17 Sept. 1995.

Note that *e-mail* is spelled with a hyphen in MLA citations.

Exercise

A. Rewrite the following sentences to add MLA-style in-text citations.

1. After the fact, however, Johanson and Edey admitted, "Neither of us was prepared for the explosion of interest that followed the formal disclosure of *afarensis* in print."

    The quotation is from page 294 of Donald Johanson and Maitland Edey's book *Lucy: The Beginnings of Humankind* (New York: Simon & Schuster, 1990).

2. In Samoa during the 1930s, girls separated socially from their siblings at about age seven and began to form close and lasting relationships with other girls their age.

    The reference is to Margaret Mead's discussion in *Coming of Age in Samoa,* originally issued in 1928 and reprinted in 1961 by Morrow Publishers in their Morrow Quill paperback series. It cites the general discussion in Chapter 5, "The Girl and Her Age Group," on pages 59 through 73 of the 1961 edition.

B. Create a list of works cited using MLA style, and include the following items.

1. An article reviewing books on Latin American families. The author is Elizabeth Anne Kuzenesof. Her review is titled "The History of the Family in Latin America." It appeared in the Spring 1989 issue

of *Latin American Research Review* on pages 168–189 (paginated by issue). This issue of the journal was number 2 in volume 24.

2. An interview of Donald Davis published in the October 1992 edition (volume 67) of the *Wilson Library Bulletin*. The interviewer was Judith O'Malley, and the interview appeared on pages 52 and 53. The periodical appears monthly.

3. A book of 280 pages by Vera Rosenbluth titled *Keeping Family Stories Alive*. The subtitle is *A Creative Guide to Taping Your Family Life and Lore*. It was published in 1990 by Hartley and Marks, a publisher in Point Roberts, Washington.

4. A collection of the stories of Shalom Aleichem titled *Around the Table: Family Stories of Shalom Aleichem*. The collection was edited by Aliza Shevron and translated by her. The book was illustrated by Toby Gowing. Scribner Publishers in New York issued the book in 1991. It contains 364 pages.

5. A scholarly article by Beverly Whitaker Long and Charles H. Grant III in volume 41 of the journal *Communication Education*. Volume 41 is dated 1992, and the article runs from page 89 to page 108. The title of the article is "The 'Surprising Range of the Possible': Families Communicating in Fiction."

49e Sample MLA paper

The following paper was written by a student using the MLA documentation style. The *MLA Handbook* recommends beginning a research paper with the first page of the text, using the format shown on Shane Hand's first page. Because his teacher required a title page and an outline as well, he prepared both of these, too. In the margins of the paper is a running commentary on the elements of the paper, from considerations of audience and purpose to organizational strategy, style, and format.

Title page
optional

Title catches readers'
attention

Place title one-third of the way down the page

Waste Disposal:

Have We Put Ourselves in Jeopardy?   *Center and double-space all lines*

by

Shane Hand   *Double-space twice between groups of lines*

Professor Charlotte Smith

English 1105

6 May 1999   *Note form of date*

Heading for all pages: last name, one space, page number (Roman numerals for outline, Arabic for paper) Hand i

Outline optional; check with instructor

Center heading

Outline

Double-space below heading

<u>Thesis statement</u>: Using landfills as a way to *Keep thesis* dispose of solid and hazardous wastes is no longer a *statem* valid option because we now know of the potential *short-on* long-term dangers to our soil and groundwater that *sentenc* landfills represent. We must both find new technologies that safely dispose of waste and reduce our own consumption.

or two

Outline uses sentences (rather than topics or phrases); ask instructor's preference

    I. Mainly two types of waste pollute our environment: solid and hazardous (toxic).

       A. Most solid waste consists of packaging residues: aluminum cans, glass and plastic bottles, paperboard cartons, and wooden crates.

       B. Most hazardous waste consists of chemical toxins, by-products of manufacturing processes, or ingredients in a wide range of products.

   II. Americans are finally becoming aware of the problems with dumping wastes in landfills.

       A. Space is the most obvious problem--people do not want a landfill in their local area.

       B. Pollution of soil and groundwater is a more threatening problem.

Hand ii

III. The key to solving the waste disposal problem
     is public commitment.
     A. People should take political action.
        1. They should urge politicians to pass
           recycling regulations.
        2. They should force businesses to become
           environmentally responsible.

Align all entries of same level

        3. They should work to develop local and
           national recycling programs.
     B. People should change their own consumer
        habits.
  IV. A poll shows that most people already have
      changed their consumer habits.
   V. Along with public commitment, new waste
      disposal technologies must also be developed.
      A. Currently, landfills with clay and plastic
         linings reduce leakage into groundwater.
      B. Currently, incineration reduces the amounts
         and toxicity of hazardous wastes.
      C. New technology should not give anyone the
         excuse not to change consumption habits.
         Recycling is still the best approach to
         solving this problem.

1/2" from top

Hand 1

1" from top of page

Shane Hand

Professor C. Smith

English 1105

6 December 1999

Put information here if you do not include title page

Double-space heading and paper

1" margin on each side

Opens with attention-getting device; reader asks, "What is it?"

Waste Disposal: Have We Put Ourselves in Jeopardy?

Indent five paces

1   A museum in New Jersey is dedicated to it. In California, artists use it to create high-priced sculpture. But no one, absolutely no one, wants to have garbage in his or her backyard. For decades we have buried it and hoped it would just disappear. But banishing it from sight did not get rid of it. Now our sins as a consumer society have come back to haunt us.

Uses we to identify with readers

2   There are many types of wastes polluting our environment. Simply put, they include municipal solid wastes and hazardous wastes. Both of these are a huge problem in the United States. They generally take up space or create a dangerous chemical imbalance. Sometimes both can happen, depending on the waste. Our soils are suffering from these pollutants, and we ourselves are in jeopardy.

Presents topic an stance

3   Solid waste, commonly known as garbage or refuse, is what for years we have calmly thrown away, confidently believing that, by some miracle, it will be collected and will disappear. A significant portion of the solid waste problem stems from packaging residues, specifically containers. Aluminum cans, glass and plastic bottles, paperboard cartons, and wooden crates are

Elaborat on ¶2 Adds definiti

1" bottom margin

Hand 2

thrown away in massive numbers, never to be used
again. An average landfill today consists of six

Adds
facts and main types of trash. Paper takes up about 50 percent
statistics by volume; plastic covers are close to 10 percent;

metals take up 6 percent; glass holds 1 percent;

organic materials cover about 13 percent; and about

Cites 20 percent is miscellaneous substances (Rathje 116).
author
and page These numbers may seem meaningless, but when we

think about the nation's daily output of these

materials (500,000 tons), it becomes clear that the

landfills are filling very quickly, so fast that our

soils cannot degrade the waste fast enough to

balance the space with the input. In fact, some

pollutants never degrade.

Defines **4**   The average person assumes that hazardous
d waste wastes account for a small percentage of today's
in larger environmental problems. However, hazardous wastes
context
are generated by almost all sectors of the economy.

These wastes are a general consequence of the

industrialized society in which we live. They

reflect our need for packaging, appliances, cleaning

supplies, beauty aids, pharmaceuticals, and other

manufactured products. As with solid wastes, for

many years toxic wastes were considered safely gone

as soon as they were carted out of sight; as one

report reminds us, however, "As with other

environmental concerns, it is only within the past

twenty to thirty years that the possible adverse

environmental quality and health problems have been

Hand 3

Uses title in citation; author unknown

recognized and addressed" (<u>Hazardous Waste</u> 3). In

the past, hazardous waste disposal was accomplished

in the quickest and least costly manner, frequently

by open dumping and uncontrolled burning. These

practices have been found to present a hazard to

human health and the environment. The magnitude of

this problem can be best presented by totaling the

amount of hazardous wastes produced each year, which

the Office of Technology Assessment puts at about

250 million metric tons (5). As our industrial   *Cites source*
                                                   second time;
society grows, finding ways to eliminate these   *page*

wastes while allowing the same or an improved   *number only*

standard of living should be an overall goal.
                                                   Uses
5   When the land was young, it was wide-open and *generaliza-*
                                                   to shift -
unspoiled. Yet as the population grew, the spoilage *definition;*

grew. But the problem has now reached such magnitude *argume*

that Americans are finally becoming concerned about

what happens to their refuse. To some extent this

concern is due to some misconceptions about the

viability of continued landfilling of municipal

solid wastes. One misconception is that the United

States is running out of landfill space. This does

not appear to be the case, as argued by a recent

study done on landfills. According to the study, "at
Uses expert source
                                                   Uses brackets
        the current rate of landfilling, all the MSW
to make key point   *to set off*
        [municipal solid waste] generated by the country *added*

        over the next thousand years could easily be *explanation*

        contained within a 30-by-30 mile area using current

        landfill technology" (Wiseman 9). However, this does

                Long quotation might have been paraphrased

Hand 4

not resolve the problem since this idea is
impractical. The space problem is distinctly
regional, and no one region will consent to be the
site for such a landfill. And where landfill siting
is most a problem--along the northeastern seaboard,
for instance--it is more often due to political
opposition than to a lack of available space. This
opposition goes back to the "not in my backyard"
syndrome.

es from
topic of
pace to
topic of
mental
damage
6   Space is not the only problem these landfills
have. There is a grave threat to the environment
through the creation of leachate. Leachate is
created when surface water contributes to the large
amount of water already existing in solid waste. The
water percolates through landfills, releasing toxic
constituents and heavy metals into soil and
groundwater. Leachate is not only dangerous but also
expensive since it must be collected, conveyed,
stored, treated, and disposed of (Organic). It also
has the potential to generate gases, including
methane, that could have long-term environmentally
destructive effects. A more immediate threat is that
the gases could cause spontaneous explosions and
fires. Even ordinary household items, once they are
in landfills, can become hazardous wastes. A

Makes
mation
eal" to
eaders
seemingly innocent bottle of nail polish puts more
than six toxic chemicals into a landfill. All of
these toxic constituents take hundreds and even
thousands of years to disappear.

7   The key to solving the waste problem once and for all is public commitment. The public should urge the politicians to pass recycling regulations and force businesses to become environmentally responsible. Public action must be taken to develop and institute recycling programs on the local and national level. Some may argue that recycling programs are expensive and thus not practical, but isn't our environment more important than a price tag? In other countries, such as Germany, recycling efforts have increased as much as 40 percent (Rathje 120). Funding for these programs comes from the government with the approval of the taxpayers (121). The public can also make a commitment even on a small scale. As seen in the above breakdown of a landfill's contents, at least 50 percent of a landfill's space is occupied by items that can be recycled. Reusing products and refusing to buy products that are not recyclable or do not contain recycled materials are two ways we as consumers can bring about change. All of these ideas will help control the space problem and relieve our soils. These kinds of efforts could be encouraged by local, state, and federal governments by increased tax incentives akin to tax reduction programs in place that spur the cleanup and redevelopment of brownfields (Pennsylvania).

8   With these ideas in mind, I turned to the public to find out whether any of these ideas were

Presents part of pronged proposal

Specifies public commitm

practiced or acceptable. I used a survey (Hand, see
appendix) which consisted of a series of questions
to find out people's habits and attitudes. My
results are based on a collection of roughly three
Places hundred responses. The participants in this survey
complete were either from the Virginia Tech area or from a
key form
appendix subdivision in Upper Marlboro, Maryland (my
it does hometown). Their ages ranged from about seventeen to
disrupt
argument fifty years old, which provided a wide range for the
average consumer. Upon tabulating the responses, I
obtained the following results.

Results
could also
be in a
table or
graph

Already Do

Use coffee mugs instead of polystyrene cups   55%

Reuse plastic wrap, foil, and plastic bags   64%

Recycle newspapers and magazines   46%

Recycle glass   57%

Recycle plastic containers   38%

Recycle aluminum cans   65%

Willing to Do

Take own bags to the store   66%

Shop at a store that's harder to get to
    but carries biodegradable products   59%

Recycle plastic containers   59%

Pay more for products in low-waste
    packaging   55%

Pay more for recycled paper   54%

9   It is important to remember that this survey
represents only a small region of the United States.

Hand 7

These results could be different in other parts of the country. It is also possible that my respondents wanted to make themselves out to be more environmentally responsible citizens than they really are. Still, I was favorably surprised by my results. It seems that many people do take some steps to preserve the environment and are willing to take other steps once they are made aware of them. This demonstrates how important it is to educate the public about the environment.

Caution about re... helps ma... presenta... seem balanced

10   Of course, along with public commitment, there must be technological improvement of waste disposal. Space and toxicity problems in landfills can be overcome or minimized by state-of-the-art landfill technology. Landfills lined with clay interposed between multiple layers of plastic sheeting greatly reduce the risk of contaminating the groundwater, especially if they are equipped with a system that collects and treats the substances that filter to the bottom of the landfill. Such a system does not need continuous removal of the substance since "landfills have an inherent capacity to lessen the toxicity of the substances introduced or generated in them" (Wiseman 9). This reduction in toxicity can also be accelerated by maintaining landfills as "biochemical" systems. As for the gases created, they can be collected and even marketed as fuel.

Presents second part of proposal

Specifies technolog... that cou... be develo... further

11   The preferred method for management of hazardous wastes is waste elimination. If wastes are not generated as the result of residential,

Reconnects to first proposal

Hand 8

commercial, and industrial actions, disposal is not
necessary. If waste is not eliminated, then steps
should be taken to reduce the amount generated. As a
result of extensive research efforts in the past few
years, more is known about incineration technology
than any of the other waste management alternatives.
For one, incineration provides a high level of toxic
control. The by-product--ash--takes up little space
in a landfill. On the other hand, when the ash by-
product of incineration is placed in a landfill, it
returns some heavy metals and other harmful organic
compounds to the soil (Montague). In addition to the
possible threat to the soil, many suspect that
incineration emissions may contribute to health
problems such as Down syndrome, asthma, and other
respiratory problems in humans as well as premature
deaths and deformaties in farm animals (Farley).
Nevertheless, incineration should probably play an
increasing role in hazardous waste management.

*Specifies
another
technology*

12   Still, though new advances in waste management
technology are moving toward resolving this
environmental problem, they do not give anybody the
excuse not to recycle since recycling is far more
beneficial to the environment than any technology.
We, as individuals, neighborhoods, and communities,
need to urge, by example and by political action,
the federal government to act now. Together, we can
clean up our garbage mess so our country can once
again be healthy and beautiful. We owe it to
ourselves as well as to future generations.

*Repeats
need to
change
habits in
conclusion*

*uses we
and our to
strengthen
appeal to
readers*

Page num continue

1/2" from top

Hand 9

↑
↓ *1" from top of page*

First line of entry not indented Works Cited   *Center heading*
Additional lines indented five spaces

Farley, Rose. "Bottom of the Ninth: Permit Hearings *List source*

mentioned paper

Double-spa

Begin in TXI's Quest to Become the Nation's

Largest Toxic Waste Incinerator." 12-18 Feb.

1998. <u>Dallas News Observer</u>. 19 Jan. 1999

⟨http://www.dallasobserver.com/archives/1998/

021298/news2.html?cat=nfc&query =TXI⟩.

Hand, Shane. Questionnaire on Consumer Habits and

Attitudes Toward Recycling. Blacksburg, VA, and

Upper Marlboro, MD. 21-25 Feb. 1999.

<u>Hazardous Waste Incineration</u>. New York: American

Society of Mechanical Engineers, 1988.

Montague, Peter. "New Study Shows Incinerator Ash More

Dangerous Than We Realized." 29 Aug. 1988.

<u>Rachel's Hazardous Waste News</u> 92. 19 Jan. 1999

⟨http://www.enviroweb.org/pubs/rachel/rhwn092.htm⟩.

Organic Waste Technologies Inc. "Leachate

Evaporation." 19 Jan. 1999

⟨http://www.owtinc.com/leachate_1.htm⟩.

Pennsylvania Department of Environmental Protection.

"Brownfields Tax Incentive." 19 Jan. 1999

⟨http://www.dep.state.pa.us/dep/deputate/

airwaste/wm/landrecy/Tax/tas.htm⟩.

Rathje, William L. "Once and Future Landfills."

<u>National Geographic</u> May 1991: 116-34.

Wiseman, Clark A. "Impediments to Economically

Efficient Solid Waste Management." <u>Resources</u>

105 (1991): 9-11.

Hand 10

Works Consulted

Brown, Kirk W. <u>Hazardous Waste and Treatment</u>.

    Woburn: Butterworth, 1983.

Bugher, Robert D. <u>Municipal Refuse Disposal</u>.

    Danville: Interstate, 1970.

Farley, Rose. "Bottom of the Ninth: Permit Hearings

    Begin in TXI's Quest to Become the Nation's

    Largest Toxic Waste Incinerator." 12-18 Feb.

    1998. <u>Dallas News Observer</u> 19 Jan. 1999

    ⟨http://www.dallasobserver.com/archives/1998/

    021298/news2.html?cat=nfc&query =TXI⟩.

Includes
all works Flack, J. E. <u>Man and the Quality of His Environment</u>.
consulted
en if not   Boulder: U of Colorado P, 1967.
cited in Hand, Shane. Questionnaire on Consumer Habits and
he paper
    Attitudes Toward Recycling. Blacksburg, VA and

    Upper Marlboro, MD. 21-25 Feb. 1999.

<u>Hazardous Waste Incineration</u>. New York: American

    Society of Mechanical Engineers, 1988.

Montague, Peter. "New Study Shows Incinerator Ash

    More Dangerous Than We Realized." 29 Aug. 1988.

    <u>Rachel's Hazardous Waste News</u> 92. 19 Jan. 1999

    ⟨http://www.enviroweb.org/pubs/rachel/rhwn092

    .htm⟩.

Organic Waste Technologies Inc. "Leachate

    Evaporation." 19 Jan. 1999 ⟨http://www.owtinc

    .com/leachate_1.htm⟩.

Pennsylvania Department of Environmental Protection.

    "Brownfields Tax Incentive." 19 Jan. 1999

Hand 11

⟨http://www.dep.state.pa.us/dep/deputate/
airwaste/wm/landrecy/Tax/tas.htm⟩.

Rathje, William L. "Once and Future Landfills."
National Geographic May 1991: 116-34.

Van Tassel, Alfred J. Environmental Side Effects of
Rising Industrial Output. Lexington: Heath,
1970.

Wiseman, Clark A. "Impediments to Economically
Efficient Solid Waste Management." Resources
105 (1991): 9-11.

Appendix

Intro:

My name is Shane and I am taking a survey in order to study the habits of the average consumer. I am interested in seeing how your habits affect the environment. Please take a few moments to answer some questions.

Survey: *Includes clean copy of any survey, questionnaire, or other primary research document*

Do you . . .

Use coffee mugs instead of		
polystyrene cups?	Yes	No
Reuse plastic wrap, foil, and		
plastic bags?	Yes	No
Recycle newspapers and/or magazines?	Yes	No
Recycle glass?	Yes	No
Recycle plastic containers?	Yes	No
Recycle aluminum cans?	Yes	No

Are you willing to . . .

Take your own bags to the store?	Yes	No
Shop at a store that's harder to get to		
but carries biodegradable products?	Yes	No
Recycle plastic containers?	Yes	No
Pay more for products in low-waste		
packaging?	Yes	No
Pay more for recycled paper?	Yes	No

CHAPTER

2

Documenting Sources: APA

The documentation style developed by the APA (American Psychological Association) identifies the source of information, ideas, or quotations by providing the author's name and the date of publication for the source within the parentheses. For this reason, APA style is often called a name-and-date style. The information in the parenthetical citation enables readers to locate more detailed information about the source in a **reference list** at the end of a paper or report.

Many writing situations call for either the APA style or a name-and-date style loosely based on the APA style but adapted to the needs of specific audiences. APA style can be easily modified and lends itself to informal uses; as a result, it is an important resource for writers looking for a direct, simple documentation system that does not disrupt the reading of a text with detailed information or by requiring readers to turn to a foot- or endnote.

USE **APA** STYLE IN . . .

ACADEMIC SETTINGS

When writing in social science fields such as psychology, sociology, business, economics, education, and political science.

For publications or professional groups requiring use of APA style.

When writing papers for an instructor who requests documentation in a name-and-date style.

WORK AND PUBLIC SETTINGS

For readers whose professions are linked to academic fields in the social sciences (personnel managers, social workers, or school administrators, for example).

continued

Use APA Style in, *(continued)*
>   When you are drawing heavily on research in the social sciences to support your paper.
>
>   When writers or publications addressing audiences similar to yours regularly use APA style or a modified form of the style.

Consider Using APA Style (perhaps in a modified form) in . . .

WORK SETTINGS
>   In business, because many business audiences prefer a name-and-date system, in part because it indicates how current the writer's sources are. (Professional audiences often have similar expectations.)

PUBLIC SETTINGS
>   When you need a simple, direct system to identify your source and its date.

APA documentation style makes the year of publication part of an in-text citation, as in (*Tannen, 1998*), and gives the date right after the author's name in a reference list to which the in-text citation refers.

```
Tannen, D. (1998). The argument culture: Moving
     from debate to dialogue. New York: Random
     House.
```

For more detailed discussion of this documentation style, consult the *Publication Manual of the American Psychological Association* (4th ed., 1994).

2a Using in-text citations

The APA system provides parenthetical citations for quotations, paraphrases, summaries, and other information in the text of a paper. For advice on what to document and what not to document, see 46a. For an APA in-text citation, you include the author's name and the year of publication, separating these items with a comma. You may choose to name the author (and give the date) either within the parenthetical citation or within your text.

Author's name inside parentheses. Include the author's name and the year of publication inside parentheses, separating these items with a comma. When you are documenting the source of a quotation, follow the date with a comma, *p.* or *pp.*, and the page number on which the quoted material appears in the source.

One recent study points out that while "women radio news directors have exceeded the men in yearly salary, that may not be the case in other radio news positions" (Cramer, 1993, p. 161).

To indicate the specific location of information or the source of paraphrased or summarized material, give the page number of the source.

In the mid-1960s, Tom Wolfe began writing unconventional and insight-filled essays about American popular culture. Despite his Ph.D. in American Studies from Yale, Wolfe and his work were at first ignored by most intellectuals, both inside and outside universities, who viewed serious or high-brow culture as far more important than popular culture (Aronowitz, 1993, p. 198).

Author's name as part of discussion. When you make an author's name part of the discussion, give the date of the source in parentheses after the name. For quoted or paraphrased material, provide the page number in the source within parentheses following the quotation or paraphrase.

As Cramer (1993) points out, "Although women radio news directors have exceeded the men in yearly salary, that may not be the case in other radio news positions" (p. 161).

When you supply the author's name and the date in your text or in an in-text citation, your readers will be able to identify a source in the list of references you provide at the end of your paper.

2b Using content footnotes

Occasionally you may wish to expand information presented in the text or discuss a point further without making the main text of your paper more complicated or harder to follow. A content footnote allows you to do this, but you should use such footnotes sparingly because too many footnotes or long footnotes can distract your readers.

To prepare a content footnote, place a number slightly above the line of your text that relates to the footnote information. Make sure that you number the footnotes in your paper consecutively.

TEXT OF PAPER   I tape-recorded all the interviews and later transcribed the relevant portions.[1]

On a separate page at the end of your paper, below the centered heading "Footnotes," present the notes in the order in which they appear in your text. Begin each note with its number, placed slightly above the line. Indent five to seven spaces, the same as a paragraph, for the first line only of each footnote, and double-space all notes.

FOOTNOTE   ¹Sections of the recordings were hard to hear and understand because of problems with the tape recorder or background noises. These gaps did not substantially affect information needed for the study.

Your instructor may prefer that you type any footnote at the bottom of the page with the text reference.

2c Creating APA in-text citations

Guide to APA Formats for In-Text Citations

1. **One Author**
2. **Two Authors**
3. **Three to Five Authors**
4. **Six or More Authors**
5. **Corporate or Group Author**
6. **No Author Given**
7. **Specific Page or Section**
8. **Work Cited More than Once**
9. **Authors with the Same Last Name**
10. **Two or More Sources in a Citation**
11. **Personal Communications, Including Interviews and Email**

---

1. One Author

Supply the author's last name and the date of the publication in parentheses, separated by a comma and a space. If the author's name appears in the text, give only the date in parentheses. If both the name and the date are included in the text, no other information need be cited.

Mallory's 1995 study of magnet schools confirmed several of the trends proposed earlier (Jacobson, 1989) and also updated the classification by Bailey (1991) based on district demographics.

2. Two Authors

Include both names in citations. In a parenthetical reference, separate the names by an ampersand (&); in the text, use the word *and*.

Part-time workers are usually paid an hourly wage rather than a salary (Mellor & Haugen, 1986). Durstan and Frank (1992) have reviewed the rates at which wages have increased in several major employment fields that include many part-timers.

3. Three to Five Authors

Include all the authors' names, separated by commas, for the first citation. For parenthetical citations use an ampersand (&) rather than *and*.

Biber, Conrad, and Reppen (1998) point out that "the language you use to write a term paper is different from the language you use when talking to your roommate" (p. 135).

In the second and other following references, give only the first author's name followed by *et al.* (for example, "Biber et al. (1998) present evidence that . . .").

4. Six or More Authors

Give the name of the first author followed by *et al.* in all citations: (*Lichtenberg et al., 1998*). Supply the names of all authors in the reference list at the end of your report.

5. Corporate or Group Author

Spell out the name of an association, corporation, or government agency for the first citation, following with an abbreviation of a cumbersome name within brackets. You may use the abbreviation for later citations.

FIRST CITATION   Depression has a number of different causes, some psychological and some physiological or organic (National Institute of Mental Health [NIMH], 1981.)

LATER CITATION   The treatments for depressive disorders vary according to the duration and intensity of the condition (NIMH, 1981).

6. No Author Given

Give the title or the first few words of a long title (*The Great Utopia: The Russian and Soviet Avant-Garde, 1915–1932* might appear in a citation as *Great Utopia*).

Art and design in 1920s Russia mixed aesthetically startling images with political themes and an endorsement of social change (*Great Utopia*, 1992).

7. Specific Page or Section

Indicate the part of the work you are citing: *p.* (for "page"); *chap.* ("chapter"), *fig.* ("figure"), for example. Spell out any words that may be confusing.

> Teenagers who survive suicide attempts experience stages of recovery, and these stages have distinct symptoms (Mauk & Weber, 1991, Table 1).

8. Work Cited More than Once

When you cite the same source more than once in a paragraph, repeat the source as necessary to clarify a specific page reference or show which information comes from one of several sources. If a second reference is clear, do not repeat the date.

> Personal debt has become a significant problem in the past decade. Much of the increase can be linked to the lack of restraint in spending people feel when using credit cards (Schor, 1998, p. 73). The problem is so widespread that "about one-third of the nation's population describe themselves as either heavily or moderately in financial debt" (Schor, p. 72).

9. Authors with the Same Last Name

When your reference list contains works by two different authors with the same last name, provide each author's initials for each in-text citation, both for works by a single author and for works by several authors.

> Scholars have looked in depth at the development of African American culture during slavery and reconstruction (E. Foner, 1988). The role of Frederick Douglass in this process has also been examined (P. Foner, 1950).

10. Two or More Sources in a Citation

If you are summarizing information found in more than one source, include all the sources—names and years—within the citation. Separate the authors and years with commas; separate the sources with semicolons. List sources alphabetically by author (as in your list of references; see p. 701), then oldest to most recent for several sources by the same author.

> Several researchers have found that work performance is affected by personality (Furnham, 1992; Gilmer, 1961, 1977).

11. Personal Communications, Including Interviews and Email

In your text, cite letters, memos, interviews, email, telephone conversations, and similar personal communications by giving the initials and last name of the person, the phrase *personal communication*, and the date. Readers probably will have no access to such sources, so you need not include them in your reference list.

AUTHOR NAMED IN TEXT	According to J. M. Hostos, the state has begun cutting funding for social services duplicated by county agencies (personal communication, October 7, 1995).
PARENTHETICAL REFERENCE	The state has begun cutting funding for social services duplicated by county agencies (J. M. Hostos, personal communication, October 7, 1995).

2d Creating an APA reference list

Immediately after the last page of your paper, you need to provide a list of references to enable readers to identify and consult the sources you have cited in your report.

- **Page format.** One inch from the top margin of a separate page at the end of your report's text (before notes or appendixes), center the heading "References" without underlining or quotation marks.
- **Alphabetizing.** List works cited in the report alphabetically by author or by the first main word of the title if there is no author. Arrange two or more works by the same author from the oldest to the most recent according to year of publication.
- **Spacing.** Double-space all entries and between entries.
- **Indentation.** Do not indent the first line, but indent five to seven spaces for the second and additional lines. *Note:* APA advises indenting the first line of a reference, not the following lines, if you are preparing a paper for publication because publications will adjust the indentation in the printed version. APA also suggests modifying this practice for student papers. We recommend indenting the second and subsequent lines for student papers because readers then can easily see the alphabetical order of the references. Be sure to check your instructor's preferences in academic settings or consider audience preferences when adapting the APA style to work or public settings.

Guide to APA Formats for References

1. Books and Works Treated as Books

1. One Author
2. Two or More Authors
3. Corporate or Group Author
4. No Author Given
5. More than One Work by the Same Author
6. More than One Work by the Same Author in the Same Year
7. One or More Editors
8. Translator
9. Edition Other than the First
10. Reprint
11. Multivolume Work
12. Anthology or Collection of Articles
13. *Diagnostic and Statistical Manual of Mental Disorders*
14. Encyclopedia or Reference Work
15. Unpublished Dissertation
16. Government Document

2. Articles and Selections from Books

17. Article in Journal Paginated by Volume
18. Article in Journal Paginated by Issue
19. Special Issue of Journal
20. Article in Popular Magazine (Weekly or Biweekly)
21. Article in Popular Magazine (Monthly)
22. Article with No Author Given

23. Article in Newspaper
24. Letter to the Editor or Editorial
25. Interview—Published
26. Review with a Title
27. Review Without a Title
28. Article from Encyclopedia or Reference Work
29. Chapter in Edited Book or Selection in Anthology
30. Dissertation Abstract

3. Other Printed and Field Resources

31. Report
32. Interview—Unpublished
33. Personal Communication
34. Paper Presented at a Meeting
35. Unpublished Raw Data

4. Media and Electronic Resources

36. Film or Videotape
37. Television or Radio Program
38. Recording
39. Database or Information Service
40. Online Source or Archived Listserv
41. World Wide Web Page
42. Online Scholarly Article
43. Online Newspaper Article
44. Online Abstract
45. CD-ROM Abstract
46. Computer Program

1 Books and works treated as books

MODEL FORMAT FOR BOOKS AND WORKS TREATED AS BOOKS

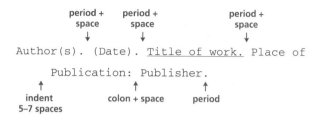

- **Author(s).** Give the author's last name followed by a comma and the initials of the first and middle names. For a book with more than one author, use the same inverted order for each author. Separate the names with commas, using an ampersand before the final name.
- **Date.** Provide the year of publication (in parentheses) followed by a period.
- **Title of work.** Give the title followed by a period, and underline both the title and the period. Use a capital only for the first word of the main title, the first word of any subtitle, and any proper nouns.
- **Publication information.** For U.S. publishers, give the city and state followed by a colon and a space; then supply the publisher's name, leaving out unnecessary words such as *Inc.* or *Publishers.* Abbreviate the name of the state using the standard postal abbreviation. You do not need to name the state for the following familiar publishing locations: Baltimore, Boston, Chicago, Los Angeles, New York, Philadelphia, and San Francisco. For publishers outside the United States, give the city and the abbreviated name of the country. No country is needed for these familiar locations: Amsterdam, Jerusalem, London, Milan, Moscow, Paris, Rome, Stockholm, Tokyo, and Vienna.
- **Spacing.** Double-space all entries, and indent five to seven spaces, the same indentation that you choose for paragraphing, for the second and any additional lines. Note that APA style advises indenting the first line of a reference, not the following lines, if you are preparing a paper for publication. Then the publication will adjust the indentation in the printed version. We recommend indenting lines following the first in your course papers because readers then can easily see the alphabetical order of the references. Be sure to ask your instructor's preferences and follow any specific directions carefully.

1. One Author

```
Wilson, W. J. (1996). When work disappears: The
    world of the new urban poor. New York:
    Knopf.
```

2. Two or More Authors

List each author's last name first, followed by first and middle initials.

```
Biber, D., Conrad, S., & Reppen, R. (1998).
    Corpus linguistics: Investigating language
    structure and use. Cambridge: Cambridge
    University Press.
```

3. Corporate or Group Author

Treat the organization or agency responsible for the work as an individual author, and alphabetize by the first main word. When author and publisher are the same, give the word *Author* following the place of publication instead of repeating the name.

```
U.S. Department of Commerce. (1996). Statistical
    abstract of the United States. Washington,
    DC: U.S. Government Printing Office.
```

4. No Author Given

Give the title first, then the date. Use the first significant word of the title to alphabetize the entry.

```
Boas anniversary volume: Anthropological papers
    written in honor of Franz Boas. (1906).
    New York: Stechert.
```

5. More than One Work by the Same Author

List works in chronological order. Include the author's name in each entry.

```
Aronowitz, S. (1973). False promises: The
    shaping of the American working class. New
    York: McGraw-Hill.
```

```
Aronowitz, S. (1993) Roll over Beethoven: The
     return of cultural strife. Hanover, NH:
     Wesleyan University Press.
```

If the same lead author has works with different co-authors, alphabetize these entries based on the last names of the second authors.

6. More than One Work by the Same Author in the Same Year

List in alphabetical order works appearing in the same year by the same author. Add lowercase letters after dates (e.g., *1992a, 1992b*). Alphabetize by the first main word in the title. For in-text citations, provide both the date and the letter (*Gould, 1987b*).

```
Gould, S. J. (1987a). Time's arrow, time's
     cycle: Myth and metaphor in the discovery
     of geological time. Cambridge, MA: Harvard
     University Press.
Gould, S. J. (1987b). An urchin in the storm:
     Essays about books and ideas. New York:
     Norton.
```
Alphabetized under *urchin*, not *An*.

7. One or More Editors

Include (*Ed.*) or (*Eds.*) after the name(s) of the editors.

```
Beckman, L., & Harvey, S. M. (Eds.). (1998).
     The new civil war: The psychology,
     culture, and politics of abortion.
     Washington, DC: American Psychological
     Association.
```

8. Translator

Include the translator's name, in normal order, after the title, followed by *Trans.*

```
Leontev, A. N. (1978). Activity, consciousness,
     and personality (M. J. Hall, Trans.).
     Englewood Cliffs, NJ: Prentice Hall.
```

9. Edition Other than the First

Include information about the specific edition in parentheses after the title (for example, *Rev. ed.* for "revised edition" or *3d ed.* for "third edition").

Gilmer, B. (1975). <u>Applied psychology:</u>
     <u>Adjustments in living and work</u> (Rev. ed.).
     New York: McGraw-Hill.

10. Reprint

Frankfort, H., Frankfort, H. A., Wilson, J. A.,
     Jacobsen, T., & Irwin, W. A. (1977). <u>The</u>
     <u>intellectual adventure of ancient man: An</u>
     <u>essay on speculative thought in the</u>
     <u>ancient Near East.</u> Chicago: University of
     Chicago Press. (Original work published
     1946)

11. Multivolume Work

Include the names of the editors or authors, making sure you indicate if they are editors. Then provide the inclusive years of publication. If the work is a revised edition or has a translator, give this information after the title. Then identify in parentheses the volumes you are using for your paper.

Strachey, J., Freud, A., Strachey, A., & Tyson,
     A. (Eds.). (1966-1974). <u>The standard</u>
     <u>edition of the complete psychological works</u>
     <u>of Sigmund Freud</u> (J. Strachey et al.,
     Trans.) (Vols. 3-5). London: Hogarth Press
     and the Institute of Psycho-Analysis.

12. Anthology or Collection of Articles

Give the name of the editor(s) first, followed by the abbreviation *Ed.* or *Eds.* in parentheses.

Cobley, P. (Ed.). (1996). <u>The communication</u>
     <u>theory reader.</u> London: Routledge.

```
Ghosh, A., & Ingene, C. A. (Eds.). (1991).

    Spatial analysis in marketing: Theory,

    methods and applications. Greenwich, CT:

    JAI.
```

13. *Diagnostic and Statistical Manual of Mental Disorders*

The manual known in short form as the *DSM-IV* is widely cited in fields such as psychology, social work, and psychiatry because its definitions and guidelines often have legal force and determine patterns of treatment. Because of the volume's importance, the APA *Publication Manual* recommends the following specific form for the entry.

```
American Psychiatric Association. (1994).

    Diagnostic and statistical manual of

    mental disorders (4th ed.). Washington,

    DC: Author.
```

In your text, following an initial full citation, you may use the standard abbreviations for this work: *DSM-III* (1980), *DSM-III-R* (1987), or *DSM-IV* (1994).

14. Encyclopedia or Reference Work

```
Kruskal, W. H., & Tanur, J. M. (1978).

    International encyclopedia of statistics

    (Vols. 1-2). New York: Free Press.
```

15. Unpublished Dissertation

```
Conrad, S. (1996). Academic discourse in two

    disciplines: Professional writing and

    student development in biology and

    history. Unpublished doctoral

    dissertation, Northern Arizona University,

    Flagstaff.
```

16. Government Document

```
Select Committee on Aging, Subcommittee on
        Human Services, House of Representatives.
        (1991). Grandparents' rights: Preserving
        generational bonds (Com. Rep. No. 102-
        833). Washington, DC: U.S. Government
        Printing Office.
```

2 Articles and selections from books

MODEL FORMAT FOR ARTICLES AND SELECTIONS

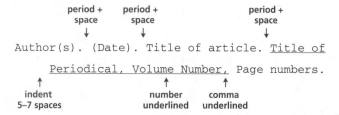

- **Author(s).** Give the author's last name and initials followed by a period and a space.
- **Date.** Supply the date in parentheses followed by a period and a space.
- **Title of article.** Give the article title, capitalizing only the first word (and the first word of any subtitle along with any proper names). Do not use quotation marks with the title. End with a period and a space.
- **Title of journal, periodical, or book.** Give the journal title (underlined, with all main words capitalized), the volume number (also underlined), and the page numbers. Use commas to separate these, and underline the comma following the title.
- **Spacing.** Double-space all entries, and indent five to seven spaces, the same indentation that you choose for paragraphing, for the second and any additional lines (see p. 57).

17. Article in Journal Paginated by Volume

You do not have to include the particular issue number because page numbers run continuously throughout the different issues making up a volume.

Eisenberg, A. R., & Garvey, C. (1981).
        Children's use of verbal strategies in
        resolving conflicts. Discourse Processes,
        4, 149-170.

Iran-Nejad, A., McKeachie, W. J., & Berliner.
        D. C. (1990). The multisource nature of
        learning: An introduction. Review of
        Educational Research, 60, 509-515.

Macklin, M.C. (1996). Preschoolers' learning of
        brand names from visual cues. Journal of
        Consumer Research, 23, 251-261.

Supply the names of all the authors in the entry in the reference list. In-text references should give only the name of the first author followed by *et al.*, as in (*Albertini et al., 1986*).

18. Article in Journal Paginated by Issue

When each issue of a journal begins with page 1, include the issue number in parentheses immediately (with no space) after the volume number. Do not underline the issue number.

Wurzbacher, K. V., Evans, E. D., & Moore, E. J.
        (1991). Effects of alternative street
        school on youth involved in prostitution.
        Journal of Adolescent Health, 12(7),
        549-554.

19. Special Issue of Journal

Begin with the special issue's editor (if other than the regular editor); otherwise, place the title at the beginning, then the date. Indicate in brackets that it is a special issue. You need not include page numbers.

Balk, D. E. (Ed.). (1991). Death and adolescent
        bereavement [Special issue]. Journal of
        Adolescent Research, 6(1).

20. Article in Popular Magazine (Weekly or Biweekly)

Supply the same information as you would for an article in a monthly magazine (see Entry 21), but add the specific date.

```
Adler, J. (1995, July 31). The rise of the

     overclass. Newsweek, 126, 33-34, 39-40,

     43, 45-46.
```
When an article is continued, list all the different pages, separated by commas.

21. Article in Popular Magazine (Monthly)

Include the month and year of the magazine. Spell out months. Add the volume number and pages. If there is no author, put the title first, before the date.

```
Dold, C. (1998, September). Needles and nerves.

     Discover, 19, 59-62.
```

22. Article with No Author Given

Begin the entry with the article's title, and alphabetize using the first main word in the title.

```
True tales of false memories. (1993, July/

     August). Psychology Today, 26, 11-12.
```

23. Article in Newspaper

Use *p.* or *pp.* to introduce the section and page numbers for newspaper articles. If no author is given, put the title first.

```
Murtaugh, P. (1998, August 10). Finding a brand's

     real essence. Advertising Age, p. 12.
```

24. Letter to the Editor or Editorial

Treat a letter to the editor like another newspaper article, but label it in brackets.

```
Bryant, K. (1995, July 16). Lawyers should push

     for early settlements of lawsuits [Letter to

     the editor]. San Jose Mercury News, p. 6C.
```

25. Interview—Published

Although APA does not specify a form for published interviews, you may wish to employ the following form, which is similar to other APA references.

Kosek, J. (1993). A different type of
    environmentalist: Ka-Kisht-Ke-Is (Chief
    Simon Lucas) [Interview]. <u>Cultural
    Survival Quarterly, 17</u>(1), 19-20.

26. Review with a Title

Following the title of the review, indicate in brackets the kind of work (*book, film, video program, television program,* and so on) and the title (underlined) of the work being reviewed.

Stolarz-Fantino, S., & Fantino, E. (1985).
    Cognition and behavior analysis [Review of
    the book <u>Judgment, decision, and choice</u>].
    <u>Journal of the Experimental Analysis of
    Behavior, 54,</u> 317-322.

27. Review Without a Title

Begin with the name of the reviewer. If the review article does not have a title, substitute a description in brackets consisting of the phrase *Review* followed by the type of material and the title of the book, film, television show, or other topic of the review.

Van Meter, E. J. (1994). [Review of the book
    <u>Preparing tomorrow's school leaders:
    Alternative-designs</u>]. <u>Educational
    Administration Quarterly, 30,</u> 112-117.

28. Article from Encyclopedia or Reference Work

If no author is identified, begin with the title of the article. Use *In* before the work's title, and follow it with the volume and page numbers.

Chernoff, H. (1978). Decision theory. In
    <u>International encyclopedia of statistics</u>
    (Vol. 1, pp. 131-135). New York: Free Press.

29. Chapter in Edited Book or Selection in Anthology

For a selection from an anthology, begin with the author's name, the year the book was published, and the title of the selection. Following the word *In,* cite the editors, the title of the collection, and the page numbers.

> Shepard, W. O. (1991). Child psychology:
>
> Identity and interaction. In J. H. Cantor,
>
> C. C. Spiker, & L. P. Lipsitt (Eds.),
>
> <u>Child behavior and developmental training</u>
>
> <u>for diversity</u> (pp. 236-257). Norwood, NJ:
>
> Ablex.

30. Dissertation Abstract

> Yamada, H. (1989). American and Japanese topic
>
> management strategies in business
>
> conversations. <u>Dissertation Abstracts</u>
>
> <u>International, 50</u>(09), 2982B.

If you consult the dissertation on microfilm, give the University Microfilms number at the end of the entry in parentheses: (*University Microfilms No. AAC--9004751*).

3 Other printed and field resources
31. Report

Begin with the name of the author, whether an individual or a group or government agency. If the agency also publishes the report, use the word *Author* in the publication information instead of repeating the group's name.

> Advisory commission to study the Consumer Price
>
> Index. (1996). <u>Toward a more accurate</u>
>
> <u>measure of the cost of living.</u> Washington,
>
> DC: Senate Finance Committee.

If the report has a number, give it in parentheses after the title with no punctuation between the title and parentheses. When several numbers are listed in the report, choose the one most likely to help readers obtain the document.

32. Interview—Unpublished

To refer to an interview you have conducted yourself, provide the information only as part of an in-text citation such as the following: (*R. Gelles, personal communication, September 14, 1993*). (See p. 55.)

33. Personal Communication

Letters, email, electronic discussion group postings, telephone conversations, and similiar communications cannot be consulted by your readers, so do not include them in your reference list. Instead, cite them in text. (See p. 55 and no.32, above for examples.)

34. Paper Presented at a Meeting

For an unpublished paper presented at a conference or symposium, include the month as well as the year, and list both the name and location of the meeting.

```
Nelson, J. S. (1993, August). Political
     argument in political science: A
     meditation on the disappointment of
     political theory. Paper presented at the
     annual meeting of the American Political
     Science Association, Chicago.
```

35. Unpublished Raw Data

When you use data from field observations, a survey, or similar kinds of research, briefly describe the contents of the data within brackets following the date. Conclude the entry with the phrase *Unpublished raw data.*

```
Williams, S. (1995). [Survey of student
     attitudes toward increased library fees].
     Unpublished raw data.
```

4 Media and electronic resources
36. Film or Videotape

Begin with the name or names of the people primarily responsible for the work, and indicate each person's role (for example, *Director* or *Producer*) in parentheses following the name. Underline the title, and then indicate the medium (for example, *film, videotape,* or *slides*) in brackets. At the end of the entry, within parentheses, indicate the location and name of the distributor (for example, *WGBH, Boston*). If the distributor is not well known, supply the address.

```
Simon, T. (Producer), & LeBrun, N. (Writer).

    (1986). Atocha: Quest for treasure

    [videotape]. (Available from Columbia

    Tristar Home Video, 3400 Riverside Drive,

    Burbank, CA 91505-4627)
```

37. Television or Radio Program

Begin the entry for a series of programs with the name of the script writer, the producer, the director, or any other person whose role you wish to indicate. Give the title of the program or series (underlined). Conclude with the location and name of the network or channel responsible for the broadcast.

```
Moyers, B. (Executive Editor). (1993). Bill

    Moyers' journal. New York: WNET.
```
Television series.

For a specific episode in a series, indicate the director in parentheses immediately following the title; then indicate the producer before the title of the series.

```
Moyers, B. A. (1993). A life together (D.

    Grubin, Director). In D. Grubin

    (Producer), Bill Moyers' journal. New

    York: WNET.
```
Single episode of television series.

38. Recording

Begin by giving the name of the writer and the date of copyright (in parentheses). Following the song title, supply the name of the recording artist in brackets, if this is someone other than the writer. Indicate the medium in brackets after the album title; include a number for the recording within the brackets if one is necessary for identifying the recording and obtaining a copy.

```
Freeman, R. (1994). Porscha [Recorded by R.

    Freeman & The Rippingtons]. On Sahara

    [CD]. New York: GRP Records.
```

39. Database or Information Service

Include the order number at the end of the citation.

Maher, F., & Tetreault, M. K. T. (1992). Inside
     feminist classrooms: An ethnographic
     approach. <u>New Directions for Teaching and
     Learning, 49,</u> 57-74. (ERIC Document
     Reproduction Service No. ED 443 234)

Schroeder, E. (1988). Therapy for the
     chemically dependent family. <u>Journal of
     Chemical Dependency Treatment</u> [On-line],
     <u>2</u>(1). Available: DIALOG File: Journal
     Chemical Dependency

Cite an abstract from an online information service (such as Lexis/Nexis) according to the following model.

Sack, K. (1995, July 14). House panel to draft
     bill requiring AIDS tests of newborns [On-
     line]. <u>The New York Times,</u> p. A15.
     Abstract from: Lexis/News/CURNWS

40. Online Source or Archived Listserv

Give the name of the author and in parentheses the date the message was posted, followed by a period. Next write the title of the message from the subject line and in brackets a description of the message. Finally, write the words *Retrieved from the World Wide Web* (or other Internet source) with the date of retrieval, a colon, and the electronic address.

Morrison, A. (1998, September 11).
     Chlorabucimil [Newsgroup posting].
     Retrieved December 20, 1998, from the
     World Wide Web: http://www.acor.org/lists/
     cancer/ws/98/09/2/0078.html

41. World Wide Web Page

Include the information specified in Entry 40.

```
Ringertz, N. (1998, December 2). Alfred Nobel's
     health and his interest in medicine.
     [Essay posted on Web site The Electronic
     Nobel Museum Project]. Retrieved December
     31, 1998, from the World Wide Web: http://
     www.nobel.se/alfred/ringertz/index.html
```

42. Online Scholarly Article

Begin with the author(s) and the date of posting. Add the title, list the source with the volume and issue numbers, and list the page numbers if given. Then indicate the medium and the date of retrieval. Conclude with the availability information needed to find the source.

```
Sheridan, J., & McAuley, J. D. (1998). Rhythm
     as a cognitive skill: Temporal processing
     deficits in autism. Noetica, 3, 8.
     Retrieved December 31, 1998, from the
     World Wide Web: http://www.cs.indiana.edu/
     Noetica/OpenForumIssue8/McAuley.html
```

43. Online Newspaper Article

Begin with as much information as possible that would be provided for a printed source. Add the words *Retrieved from the World Wide Web* and give the date of retrieval, a colon, and the electronic address.

```
Sonner, S. (1998, December 31). Psychologist
     ponders horse killer. Washington Post
     Online [Newspaper, selected stories on
     line]. Retrieved December 31, 1998, from
     the World Wide Web: http://search
     .washingtonpost.com/wp-srv/WAPO/19981231/
     V000412-123198-idx.html
```

44. Online Abstract

For an abstract, give the source of the original work and the location of the abstract.

```
Globus, G. (1995, August). Quantum
    consciousness is cybernetic [Abstract].
    PSYCHE, 2(12). Retrieved January 8, 1998,
    from the World Wide Web:
    http://psyche.cs.monash.edu.au/ v2/
    psyche-2-12-curran.html
```

45. CD-ROM Abstract

```
Schroeder, E. (1988). Therapy for the
    chemically dependent family [CD-ROM].
    Journal of Chemical Dependency, 2, 95-129.
    Abstract from: SilverPlatter File: PsycLIT
    Item: 76-37924
```

46. Computer Program

In brackets after the title, identify the source as a computer program, a computer programming language, or computer software. If the program's author owns specific rights to it, begin the entry with the author's name. Otherwise, begin with the name of the material. Give the location and name of the organization producing the program. Add any version number or retrieval information at the end in parentheses unless it is part of the title.

```
Family tree maker [Computer software]. (1993).
    Fremont, CA: Banner Blue Software.
    (Windows version)
```

Exercise

A. Turn to Exercise A in Chapter 1. Rewrite the sentences supplied there to add in-text citations in APA style.

B. Turn to Exercise B in Chapter 1. Rewrite the items supplied there to create a list of references in APA style.

C. Working with a partner or a small group, compare your answers to Exercise A and B above. Correct any errors in your answers, using your handbook or your instructor's advice to resolve any differences of opinion.

2e Sample APA Paper

Supply abbreviated title (50 characters maximum) for heading

Center title and all other lines

Supply name and institution

Ask your instructor if instructor's name, course name, and date are necessary

Running head: CYCLISTS

Cyclists 1

Number title page and all others using short title

Competitive Cyclists: Who Are They?

Steven King

University of Rhode Island

Double-space twice between groups of lines

Professor Hasan Danesh

Sociology 150

Section 10

November 24, 1998

Use short title Cyclists 2
and page number

Center heading
Abstract

Supply one ¶ and do not indent

Cyclists at a race were asked to fill out a
questionnaire about attitudes toward cycling,
demographics, and self-perception of social status.
Responses to the questionnaire provided general
support for an initial hypothesis regarding the low
level of women's participation in competitive
cycling but not for a hypothesis regarding enjoyment
of extreme physical exertion and pain as a reason
for undertaking competitive cycling. In addition,
the responses suggested further hypotheses
concerning the relative lack of participation by
cyclists under 25 years old and the likelihood that
people of different ages, marital status, and levels
of education undertake competitive cycling for
different reasons.

Double-space abstract and rest of paper

Summarize paper in no more than about 120 words

Besides the abstract, typical sections in an APA paper are Introduction, Method, Results, and Discussion

*First part is introduction
but no heading is used*

↕ *1" top margin*

Repeat and center title

*Indent ¶ five
to seven spaces;
introduction*
1.
*present
problem or
ject,
background
information,*
*thesis
guiding
stion*

Competitive Cyclists: Who Are They?   *be consistent
for ¶s and
references*

Bicycle riding is the third most popular

participant sport in the United States, with an

estimated 55.3 million people riding a bike at least

once a year (<u>Interbike,</u> 1992) for varying reasons and   *Citation
uses title*

with widely differing perspectives (Worthington, 1998; *no author*

Meyer, 1997; Zimberoff, 1996). Another report, from the

Bicycle Institute of America (1990), estimates that 25

million American adults ride a bicycle an average of

once a week. That same survey indicates that 220,000

adults took part in bicycle races during the year, or

less than 1% of those who ride frequently.

2   In this paper I report on a group of people who

*argin
ach
de*

entered a particular bicycle race. I collected data

through a survey taken at the race. The survey asked

for demographic data as well as information about

level of commitment and motivation. I then summarized

and analyzed the data. Although the purpose of my

study was primarily descriptive, I also was able to

estimate the kind of support available for two

hypotheses I developed before beginning the study. In

addition, the study suggested several more hypotheses

useful for further research.

[The introduction goes on to provide background information on
competitive cycling as a sport.]

Explains how the study was carried out   Method   *Center section heading*

*ollows
neral
PA practice,
scussing
bjects,
aterials,
and procedure for the study*

3   I gathered the data for this paper at a

bicycle race held in Westerly, Rhode Island, on

Sunday, September 27, 1998. Called "The First

Annual Charlestown 40 Kilometer Time Trial," the

↑ *1" bottom margin*

event consisted of each entrant riding the course
individually "against the clock." The course was
on smoothly paved roads and was relatively flat.
There were 37 entrants, 34 male and 3 female. *Supplies cross-reference to survey in Appendix*

4   The respondents filled out a survey (see
Appendix) after they had completed the event and
were waiting for the results. I circulated through
the parking area and asked the entrants to go to the
registration table and complete the survey. My
original plan was to have the entrants complete the
survey prior to the race at registration. My goal
was a 100% response. As it worked out, I achieved an
88% response rate (32 of 36 possible respondents; I
was the 37th entrant).

5   The questionnaire requested basic demographic
information including a question regarding self-
perception of social status. It also asked
respondents to rate their cycling ability and
indicate how many years they had been active in
cycling competition. A question about the distance
traveled to get to the race was intended to provide
some indication of the level of commitment to
cycling competition. Traveling a substantial
distance to the race involves a considerable time
commitment and willingness to pay for transportation
and meals in addition to race entry fees. A final
open-ended question asked for three to five reasons
why the respondent entered competitive cycling
events.

Provides theoretical background for study and context for   Cyclists 5
methods and conclusions; Literature Review section often follows Introduction

Literature Review

6   The factors motivating competitive cyclists do
not appear to be a major issue in sociology or
psychology at the present time. No journal articles
that deal directly with the topic were found.
Nonetheless, articles on body image, weight loss,
and health risk-taking provide useful background for
the present study.

7   In an article relating body image and exercise,
David and Cowles (1991) make interesting comparisons
between men and women and between younger and older
men. Older men (over 25) and women of all ages are
likely to desire to lose weight when asked to
consider their own bodies. Women are far more
dependent on dieting to lose weight than men, who
seem more likely to exercise. Drewnowski and Yee
(1987) also emphasize the tendency of women to turn
to dieting and of men to turn to exercise in order
to control weight. Schneider and Greenberg (1992)
found that participants in individual sports such as
swimming, jogging, tennis, and cycling tend to take
fewer behavioral health risks in other aspects of
their lives than do participants in team sports.

8   A physiological study of the determinants of
endurance in well-trained cyclists found that
cyclists with 5 or more years of cycling experience
had superior endurance compared to similarly trained
cyclists with 2 to 3 years of experience (Coyle,
Coggan, Hopper, & Walters, 1988). This study
suggests a link between performance and years of

te up
five
thors in
st reference to a work

cycling experience. Because responses to the survey were anonymous, this study was unable to test the hypothesis by linking experience to performance in the race.

Section added to discuss

Hypotheses   hypotheses in detail

9   This study was intended to be descriptive and to produce hypotheses for further research rather than test them. Nonetheless, I began the study with two tentative hypotheses designed to help interpret the data. On the basis of my experience with cycling, I predicted that the percentage of women entrants in the race would be approximately 10% and would not exceed 20%. In addition, on the basis of my experience and my reading about cycling (Matheny, 1986), I predicted that a common response to the survey question on motivation would be a half-humorous suggestion of "love of pain" or "love of suffering." Pain and suffering in fact can be powerful if complex motivators in sport. Members of one bicycling group who race to remind the public about the effects of asbestos and toxic chemicals explain:

> We tell the public that the temporary pain we experience racing bicycles is nothing like the pain a mesothelioma or cancer patient faces every hour of every day. As bike racers, we choose to suffer swollen legs and burning legs when climbing mountains or sprinting for the win. We know that a terminal asbestos patient does

> not have this choice--his pain and anguish
> was [sic] forced upon him and his family.
> We do not take our health for granted!
> (Worthington, 1998)

This study aims to discover whether motivations of
this sort are widespread.

*Provides detailed summary of
questionnaire responses*

Results

10   The gender split among respondents was 93.8%
male and 6.3% female. This closely matches the overall
registration proportion of 92.3% male and 7.7% female.
The mean age of respondents was 36.6 years, ranging
from a low of 16 to a high of 62. Only 1 entrant was
under 25 while 5 were over 50. Just under half (46.9%)
the respondents indicated they were married. No
respondents indicated a household size of 6 or more.
Education level was quite high middle class.

11   The question rating level of cycling ability
brought about a respondent-created category. Three
respondents felt so torn between the intermediate
and advanced categories that they drew a large
circle around both. If only one person had done
this, I would have made an assignment based on other
criteria, but with 3 out of 32 choosing this option,
I decided to label it an additional category. There
was also one crossed-out and re-circled response to
this question, indicating that at least one more
person had difficulty with the distinction between
the two categories.

*Detailed
information
could be
presented in table or chart*

12   The mean number of seasons involved with
competitive cycling was 4.2 years, ranging from 1 (5

cases) to 10 years (5 cases). Many of the athletes probably had experience in other aerobic sports prior to or overlapping with cycling. A high proportion (71.9%) of the respondents traveled over 50 miles one way to enter a race within the past year. Over two-thirds (69.2%) of those who traveled this distance did so with some frequency, four or more times during 1992.

13   The open-ended question regarding reasons for entering bicycle races produced 22 different *Includes results that do not support* responses. The most popular cluster was enjoyment of *hypotheses* competition at 75%, followed by enjoyment of training at 59%, friendship with other cyclists at 40%, and health benefits of cycling at 31.3%.

Analyzes results and their implications Discussion

14   In terms of the number of seasons of cycling experience, those respondents older than the mean of 36.6 years averaged exactly twice as many years' experience as those younger than the mean (5.8 years to 2.9 years). Only one cyclist (7%) over age 36 was in the first year of competition, while four (22.2%) age *Might be* 36 or under were in the first year. More of the young *organized* *more clearly* riders traveled 50 miles to a race (77% to 64%), but *to correspond* the older riders who did travel did so more frequently *with* *questionnaire* than their younger counterparts. Only 2 (11.2%) of the *items or* younger group traveled 7 or more times, compared to 6 *previous* *discussion* (42.8%) of the older group. It seems that perhaps the older group is more committed one way or the other--to travel and compete regularly or to stay home.

15   Because of the low number of female entrants/respondents, it is not appropriate to make

statistical comparisons between male and female
respondents. I will say, though, that the responses
of the 2 women who completed the survey show little
to distinguish them from the male respondents. It
may be that this particular survey did not bring out
gender-based differences, or it may be that the
cycling experience transcends gender. The data are
too slim to support even a preliminary conclusion.

plores
ationships
iong
swers,
ggesting
ntative
iclusions
d research
ues

16   Drawing on the results, I compared married
respondents to all others. I found that married
racers tend to live in larger households, with 53.3%
living in households of 3 or more versus 17.6% of
the nonmarried group. Of interest is that there are
no beginning-level cyclists among the married
respondents but 25% among the nonmarried group. It
is tempting to hypothesize that married people are
less likely to take up a new competitive sport such
as bicycle racing, but I'm restrained by personal
knowledge of many cyclists who have started
competing after being married. Married people also
mentioned health benefits as a reason for competing
more frequently than nonmarrieds (53.3% to 12.5%).
Health benefits were also more important to older
cyclists (42%) than younger cyclists (22%).

ntinues
scussion
ationships
scovered
rough
alysis of
sults

17   There was no apparent relationship between age
and marital status. The mean age of the entire sample
(36.635) and the mean age of the married cyclists
(36.60) is within .035 years. When I controlled for
marital status (married) and household size (3 or
more), I discovered a drop in the percentage that

travel from 66.7% to 50%. Both respondents who mentioned cycling as a stress release are married and in a larger household. By the same token, there was almost perfect agreement between these age and marital status subgroups and the entire sample on the two most popular reasons for competing, enjoyment of competition and enjoyment of the training process.

18 Splitting the group on the basis of level of education showed that 90% of those with no college degree traveled 50 miles to a race at least once. But only 1 (10%) mentioned racing for fun and only 1 (10%) mentioned racing for health benefits while 40% mentioned competing to achieve personal goals. Health (40%) and fun (31%) were both more important among those with a college degree while achievement of personal goals was relatively less important (13.6%).

[The discussion continues with a critique of the survey and its administration. The writer raises questions about the representativeness of the sample and the timing of the questionnaire's administration. He also discusses some problems with the phrasing of individual questions.]

Conclusions

Discusses whether the research supports hypotheses or answers guia questions

19 This study had three goals: to describe the group being studied, to test the viability of two hypotheses, and to formulate additional hypotheses. The survey responses provide a rough but interesting description of competitive cyclists and suggest that the group deserves further study.

Sums up goals of research and contributions to discussion of the sub

20 Of the two proposed hypotheses, the one regarding the level of women's participation seems likely to be supported by further research. This research also needs to look at the reasons for the

relatively low level of women's participation,
perhaps beginning with the literature suggesting
that women in general tend to depend on diet rather
than exercise to control weight. Questions of body
image and the difficulty of cycling while
overweight may also be worth considering. Other
factors having nothing to do with weight may be
significant. For instance, women may be drawn to
mountain biking more than bicycle racing because of
more equitable distribution of sponsorships, media
coverage, and prize money (Meyer, 1996). Also,
women may perceive road training for bicycle racing
as more hazardous than other sporting activities
(Zimberoff, 1996) *Might consider whether family responsibilities limit women's participation*

21   The second hypothesis regarding "love of pain"
as a reason for cycling received little support from
the data. This response was not even among the top
10 on the questionnaire. *Suggests directions for further research*

22   Several new hypotheses emerged during the study.
One deals with the low number of male competitors
under 25 years of age. It may be the case that the
health and weight concerns of men under 25 and the
benefits of competitive cycling are contradictory.
Some hypotheses regarding reasons for competing seem
worth considering. It may be that people of different
ages, marital status, and education levels have
considerably different reasons for undertaking the
same activity, in this case, racing a bicycle. These
questions are certainly worth further study.

List sources alphabetically by last name of author

Center heading

References

Coyle, E. F., Coggan, A. R., Hopper, M. K., & *Double-space*
First line Walters, T. J. (1988). Determinants of *all entries*
of entry endurance in well-trained cyclists. <u>Journal of</u>
not indented <u>Applied Physiology, 64,</u> 2622-2630.

David, C., & Cowles, M. (1991). Body image and
    exercise. <u>Sex Roles, 25,</u> 33-34.   *Additional lines indented five spaces, like*

Drewnowski, A., & Yee, D. K. (1987). Men and body *paragraphs*
    image: Are males satisfied with their body *following*
    weight? <u>Psychosomatic Medicine, 49,</u> 626-634. *instructor's directions*

<u>Interbike 1992 directory.</u> (1992). Costa Mesa, CA: *List source with*
    Primedia.   *no author by title*

Matheny, F. (1986, February 5). Solo cycling. <u>Volo</u>
    <u>News,</u> 157.

Meyer, J. (1997). Alison Sydor, cyclist, on equity
    in cycling. Reprinted from <u>ACTION</u>, Winter 1994.
    Canadian Association for the Advancement of
    Women and Sport and Physical Activity.
    Retrieved November 9, 1998, from the World Wide
    Web: http://www.makeithappen.com/wis/readings/
    insydor.htm

Schneider, D., & Greenberg, M. (1992). Choice of
    exercise: A predictor of behavioral risks.
    <u>Research Quarterly for Exercise and Sport, 9,</u>
    231-245.

Worthington, R. G. (1998). Labor power racing: Lung
    busters, leg breakers. [Announcement posted on
    the World Wide Web]. Washington, DC. Author.
    Retrieved November 9, 1998, from the World

Wide Web: http://www.mesothel.com/pages/
labpower.htm

Zimberoff, B. F. (1996). Ocean to ocean on two
wheels: Harassment on the road. <u>Armchair World
NetEscapes.</u> Retrieved November 9, 1998, from
the World Wide Web: http://www.armchair.com/
escape/ bike7.html

Center heading and name of figure or material
Add A, B, and so on to heading if more than one appendix

Appendix

Page numbers continue

Survey

Please take a minute or two to answer the following questions for a University of Rhode Island study of demographics and motivation of competitive athletes.

1. Sex (circle one) Male Female

2. Date of birth (month/day/year) __/__/__

3. Marital status (circle one)

      Married Single Divorced Widowed Other

4. Number of people in your household (circle one)

      1 2 3 4 5 6 or more

Use clear material, retyped or redrawn if necessary

5. Education level (circle one)

      Haven't finished high school

      High school or equivalency degree

      Associate degree

      Bachelor's degree

      Master's degree

      Doctoral degree

6. In regard to family income, attitudes, and values, how do you view your social status? (circle one)

      Lower class   Lower middle class

      Middle middle class   Upper middle class

      Upper class

7. How do you rate yourself as a competitive cyclist? (circle one)

      Beginner Intermediate Advanced Expert

8. How many years have you been involved in competitive cycling? _____

9. Have you traveled more than 50 miles one way to enter a bike race, triathlon, or biathlon during 1992? (circle one) Yes No
    If you answered yes to the above question, approximately how many times did you travel that far to enter an event? _____

10. Please list a few (3 to 5) reasons why you enter competitive cycling events (including biathlons and triathlons).

  I. _____

 II. _____

III. _____

 IV. _____

  V. _____

Thank you very much for completing this survey.

RIDE FAST!

3

Documenting Sources: CBE

One typical and widely used form of documentation in the natural sciences is the Council of Biology Editors (CBE) style.

USE CBE STYLE (IN ONE OF ITS VARIATIONS) IN . . .

ACADEMIC SETTINGS

When writing in natural science fields such as biology and related sciences

When writing for publications requiring use of CBE style

When writing papers for an instructor who requests CBE documentation or "some form of scientific documentation"

WORK AND PUBLIC SETTINGS

When addressing scientific issues for an audience that is reasonably expert in the field and expects you to provide current scientific knowledge

When writing for professional groups or company divisions that expect use of scientific documentation or require CBE documentation

---

CBE style tends to have more variations than the other styles, mainly because the papers written in the fields of natural science that employ **CBE documentation style** have different structural requirements. For this reason, it is important to check with your instructor or the publication or audience for which you are writing to find out which variations to use. The following discussion covers the two most common variations of CBE style. For more detailed information, see *Scientific Style and Format: The CBE Manual for Authors, Editors, and Publishers* (6th ed., 1994).

3a Creating CBE in-text citations

You can use one of two methods for CBE in-text references, the name-and-year method or the number method.

1 Use the name-and-year method

With this method, you include the name of the author or authors along with the publication year of the text. If you do not mention the author's name in the paper itself, include both the name and the year in parentheses; if you do mention the name, include only the year.

PARENTHETICAL REFERENCE

Decreases in the use of lead, cadmium, and zinc in industrial products have resulted in a "very large decrease in the large-scale pollution of the troposphere" (Boutron and others 1991, p 64).

AUTHOR NAMED IN TEXT

Boutron and others (1991) found that decreases in the use of lead, cadmium, and zinc in industrial products have resulted in a "very large decrease in the large-scale pollution of the troposphere" (p 64).

If you cite several works by the same author, all of which appeared in a single year, use letters (*a, b,* and so forth) after the date to distinguish them.

ONE OF SEVERAL APPEARING IN THE SAME YEAR

Decreases in the use of lead, cadmium, and zinc in industrial products have resulted in a "very large decrease in the large-scale pollution of the troposphere" (Boutron and others 1991a, p 64).

2 Use the number method

With this method, you use numbers instead of names of authors. The numbers can be placed in parentheses in the text or raised above the line as superscript figures. The numbers correspond to numbered works on your reference list. There are two ways to use the number method. In one style, you number your in-text citations consecutively as they appear in your paper and arrange them accordingly on the reference page.

Decreases in the use of lead, cadmium, and zinc in industrial products have reduced pollution in the troposphere (1).

In the second style, you alphabetize your references first, number them, and then refer to the corresponding number in your paper. Since only the number appears in your text, make sure you mention the author's name if it is important.

Boutron and others found that decreases in the use of lead, cadmium, and zinc in industrial products have reduced pollution in the troposphere (3).

3b Creating a CBE reference list

You may use "Cited References" or just "References" as the heading for your reference list. If your instructor asks you to supply references for all your sources, not just the ones cited in your text, prepare a second list called "Additional References," "Additional Reading," or "Bibliography."

The order of the entries in your reference list should correspond to the method you use to cite them within your paper. If you use the name-and-year method, for example, organize the references alphabetically according to the last name of the main author or chronologically by date of publication for works by the same author(s).

If you use the consecutive number method, the reference list will not be alphabetical but will be arranged according to which work comes first in your paper, which second, and so forth. If you use the alphabetized number method, arrange your list alphabetically, and then number the entries.

Following are some examples of the most commonly used formats for entries. Refer to *Scientific Style and Format: The CBE Manual* for further examples of documentation.

Guide to CBE Formats for References

1. BOOKS AND WORKS TREATED AS BOOKS

1. One Author
2. Two or More Authors
3. Corporate or Group Author
4. Editor
5. Translator
6. Conference Proceedings
7. Technical Report

2. ARTICLES AND SELECTIONS FROM BOOKS

8. Article in Journal Paginated by Volume
9. Article in Journal Paginated by Issue
10. Article with Corporate or Group Author
11. Entire Issue of Journal
12. Figure from Article
13. Selection in Anthology or Collection

3. ELECTRONIC RESOURCES

14. Patent from Database or Information Service
15. Online Article
16. Online Book
17. Online Abstract
18. CD-ROM Abstract

---

1 Books and works treated as books

Formats for entries for the name-and-year method and the number method are the same except for the location of the year. The sample entries for a reference list follow the style for the number method, but model formats are shown for both methods.

MODEL FORMAT FOR BOOKS AND WORKS TREATED AS BOOKS

NAME-AND-YEAR METHOD

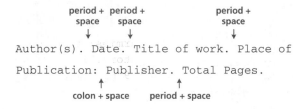

NUMBER METHOD

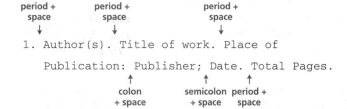

- **Author(s).** Give the author's name in inverted order, beginning with the last name and followed by *the initials only* (without periods or spaces) of the first and middle names, concluding with a period and a space. For more than one author, follow the same pattern for each author, and separate the names with a comma followed by a space. (Some scientific publications use full names for authors; check if this style is required for your paper.) If no author is given, begin with the word *Anonymous* in brackets.
- **Title of work.** Give the title followed by a period and a space. Do not underline the title, and capitalize only the first word and proper nouns or adjectives. Do not capitalize the subtitle following a colon.
- **Publication information.** Indicate the city, publisher, and date of publication. Put a colon after the city and a semicolon after the publisher. Conclude with a period. To avoid confusion between two cities with the same name or to identify cities likely to be unfamiliar, place a comma and a space after the city and include the abbreviated name of the state or the country.

- **Total pages.** Supply the total number of pages in the work, including the index, but do not add in any preliminary pages with Roman numerals.
- **Spacing.** Double-space your entries. For the name-and-year method, do not indent any lines. For the number method, begin the second and any later lines underneath the beginning of the opening word in the first line. If your instructor gives you other spacing directions, follow these carefully.

1. One Author

> 1. Simpson HN. Invisible armies: the impact of disease on American history. Indianapolis: Bobbs-Merrill; 1980. 239 p.

2. Two or More Authors

List each author's last name first, and use commas to separate the authors.

> 2. Freeman JM, Kelly MT, Freeman JB. The epilepsy diet treatment: an introduction to the ketogenic diet. New York: Demo; 1994. 180 p.

3. Corporate or Group Author

Treat an organization or government agency responsible for a work as you would an individual author. If the author is also the publisher, include the name in both places. You can use an organization's acronym in place of the author's name if the acronym is well known.

> 3. World Health Organization. Ataractic and hallucinogenic drugs in psychiatry: report of a study group. Geneva: World Health Organization; 1958. 179 p.

4. Editor

Identify the editor(s) by including the word *editor(s)* (spelled out) after the name.

> 4. Dolphin D, editor. Biomimetic chemistry. Washington: American Chemical Society; 1980. 437 p.

5. Translator

Give the translator's name after the title, followed by a comma and the word *translator.* If the work has an editor as well, place a semicolon after the word *translator* and then name the editor and conclude with the word *editor.* Give the original title at the end of the entry after the words *Translation of* and a colon.

> 5. Jacob F. The logic of life: a history of
>   heredity. Spillmann BE, translator. New
>   York: Pantheon Books; 1982. 348 p.
>   Translation of: Logique du vivant.

6. Conference Proceedings

Begin with the name of the editor(s) and the title of the publication. Indicate the name, year, and location of the conference, using semicolons to separate the information. Include the total number of pages at the end. You need not name the conference if the title does so.

> 6. Witt I, editor. Protein C: biochemical and
>   medical aspects. Proceedings of the
>   International Workshop; 1984 July 9-11;
>   Titisee, Germany. Berlin: De Gruyter; 1985.
>   195 p.

7. Technical Report

Treat a report as you would a book with an individual or corporate author, but include the total number of pages after the publication year. If the report is available through a particular agency—and it usually is—include the information a reader would need to order it. The report listed here can be obtained from the EPA department mentioned using the report number EPA/625/7-91/013. Enclose a widely accepted acronym for an agency in brackets following its name.

> 7. Environmental Protection Agency (US) [EPA].
>   Guides to pollution prevention: the
>   automotive repair industry. Washington: US
>   Environmental Protection Agency; 1991; 46 p.
>   Available from: EPA Office of Research and
>   Development; EPA/625/7-91/013.

2 Articles and selections from books

MODEL FORMAT FOR ARTICLES AND SELECTIONS

NAME-AND-YEAR METHOD

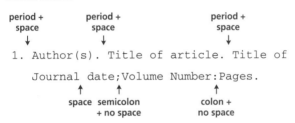

- **Author(s).** Give the author's name in inverted order, beginning with the last name and followed by the initials only (without periods or spaces) of the first and middle names, concluding with a period and a single space. For more than one author, follow the same pattern for each author, and separate the names with a comma followed by a space. If no author is given, begin with *Anonymous,* placed in brackets.
- **Title of article and publication information.** Give the article name, journal name, date, volume number and issue number (in parentheses), and page numbers. Do not enclose the article title in quotation marks or underline the journal title. Capitalize only the first word and any proper nouns in an article's title; do not capitalize the first word in a subtitle. For journal titles, follow regular capitalization rules, but use abbreviations standard in the field (see following page). Conclude the title of the article with a period and a space. Place a space but no punctuation between the title of the journal and the date. Do not include a space before or after the colon separating the volume number from the page numbers or between volume and issue numbers.

- **Pages.** Include the specific pages of the article or chapter.
- **Journal title (abbreviated).** Always abbreviate a journal title unless it is a one-word title. To find out how to abbreviate titles, notice the abbreviations used in your sources and ask your instructor which book lists abbreviations for your field.
- **Spacing.** Double-space all entries. Do not indent the first line or any subsequent lines (name and year); align second and later lines under the beginning of the initial word of the first line.

8. Article in Journal Paginated by Volume

```
8. Yousef YA, Yu LL. Potential contamination of
   groundwater from Cu, Pb, and Zn in wet
   detention ponds receiving highway runoff. J
   Environ Sci Hlth 1992;27:1033-44.
```

9. Article in Journal Paginated by Issue

Give the issue number within parentheses immediately (with no space) after the volume number.

```
9. Boutron CF. Decrease in anthropogenic lead,
   cadmium and zinc in Greenland snows since
   the late 1960's. Nature 1991;353(6340):153-
   5, 160.
```

10. Article with Corporate or Group Author

Treat the corporate or group author as you would any author. If a person's name is part of the corporation, as in this example, do not transpose the first and last names. Alphabetize by the first main word in the corporation name, even if it is a first name.

```
10. Derek Sims Associates. Why and how of acoustic
    testing. Environ Eng 1991;4(1):10-12.
```

11. Entire Issue of Journal

Include the title of the main editor or compiler of the specific issue because this person will often be a guest editor.

```
11. Savage A, editor. Proceedings of the
    workshop on the zoo-university connection:
    collaborative efforts in the conservation of
    endangered primates. Zoo Biol 1989;1(Suppl).
```

12. Figure from Article

Include the title of the figure (or table, chart, or diagram) and its number, as well as the page on which it appears. Use *p* in this context.

    12. Kanaori Y, Kawakami SI, Yairi K. Space-time
        distribution patterns of destructive
        earthquakes in the inner belt of central
        Japan. Engng Geol 1991;31(3-4):209-30 (p
        216, table 1).

13. Selection in Anthology or Collection

The first name and title refer to the article; the second name and title refer to the book from which the article is taken. Include the page numbers of the article at the end of the citation.

    13. Moro M. Supply and conservation efforts for
        nonhuman primates. In Gengozian N, Deinhardt
        F, editors. Marmosets in experimental
        medicine. Basel: S. Karger AG; 1978. p 37-40.

3 Electronic resources
14. Patent from Database or Information Service

The sample below, from the inventors' names through the date, illustrates how to cite a patent. In this instance, information about electronic access is added at the end.

    14. Collins FS, Drumm ML, Dawson DC, Wilkinson
        DJ, inventors. Method of testing potential
        cystic fibrosis treating compounds using
        cells in culture. US patent 5,434,086. 1995
        July. 18 Available from: Lexis/Nexis/Lexpat
        library/ALL file.

15. Online Article

    15. Grolmusz V. On the weak mod m representation
        of Boolean functions. Chi J Theor Comp Sci
        [serial online] 1995 July 21;100-5. 2
        screens. Available from:
        http://www.csuchicago.edu/publication/cjtcs/
        articles/1995/2/contents.html via the World
        Wide Web. Accessed 1996 May 3.

16. Online Book

16. Darwin C. 1859. On the origin of species by means of natural selection, or the preservation of favoured races in the struggle for life [book online]. London: Down, Bromley, Kent. Available from: ftp://sailor.gutenberg.org/ pub/gutenberg/ etext98/otoos10.txt via the World Wide Web. Accessed 1999 Feb 12.

17. Online Abstract

Use a form similar to that for journal articles, but give the word *abstract* in brackets following the title.

17. Smithies O, Maeda N. Gene targeting approaches to complex genetic diseases: atherosclerosis and essential hypertension [abstract]. Proc Natl Acad Sci USA 1995; 92(12):5266-72. 1 screen. Available from: Lexis/Medline/ABST. Accessed 1996 Jan 21.

18. CD-ROM Abstract

Indicate the medium (*CD-ROM*) in brackets following the title. Close the entry with the phrase *Available from*, followed by information about the source and retrieval number.

18. MacDonald R, Fleming MF, Barry KL. Risk factors associated with alcohol abuse in college students. Am J Drug and Alc Abuse [CD-ROM]; 17:439[hypehn]49. Available from: SilverPlatter File: PsycLIT Item: 79-13172.

Exercise

 A Turn to Exercise A in Chapter 1. Rewrite the sentences supplied there to add either form of in-text citations in CBE style. Prepare a corresponding list of references.

 B Turn to Exercise B in Chapter 1. Rewrite the items supplied there to create a list of references following either form used in CBE style.

 C Working with a partner or a small group, compare your answers to Exercises A and B above. Correct any errors in your answers, using your handbook or your instructor's advice to resolve any differences of opinion.

4

Documenting
Sources: CMS

The documentation style outlined in *The Chicago Manual of Style* (the CMS style) provides references in the form of endnotes or footnotes. Endnotes or footnotes are signaled by a superscript numeral in the text (for example,[1]) and a correspondingly numbered reference note at the end of the paper (an endnote) or, less often, at the bottom of the page (a footnote). A bibliography at the end of the paper provides a list of all the sources in alphabetical order. Endnotes and footnotes are less compact than parenthetical references, yet they offer you a chance to cite a source in more specific detail and to include brief explanatory material. Readers especially interested in your sources will find themselves repeatedly turning away from the text itself to consult the notes, however.

USE CMS STYLE IN . . .

ACADEMIC SETTINGS

When writing papers in history and some other fields in the arts and sciences (check with your instructor)

When writing for publications and professional groups requiring use of CMS style or a footnote/endnote style

When writing papers for an instructor who requests documentation using "Turabian" or "Chicago Manual" style or who asks for footnotes or endnotes

WORK AND PUBLIC SETTINGS

When the audience you are addressing expects you to use footnotes/endnotes or when other writers addressing the audience generally use footnotes or endnotes

continued

USE CMS STYLE IN ... *(continued)*

CONSIDER USING CMS STYLE (PERHAPS IN A MODIFIED FORM) IN ...
WORK AND PUBLIC SETTINGS

When you do not wish to distract readers by including author's names,
page numbers, or dates of your sources throughout the text and
when you recognize that your readers will not find it necessary to
consult every note as they read

4a Using endnotes and footnotes

To indicate a reference in the body of your text, insert a number
slightly above the line[2], making sure you number the references consecutively. Insert a number to indicate a reference to the source of a quotation,
to alert readers to specific information and ideas borrowed from a source,
or to specify the source of paraphrased or summarized material. At the
end of the paper (in an endnote) or at the bottom of the page (in a footnote), provide detailed information about the source.

TEXT OF PAPER
> To emphasize how isolated and impoverished his child-
> hood neighborhood was, Wideman describes it as being
> not simply on "the wrong side of the tracks" but actually
> "under the tracks, if the truth be told—in a deep hollow
> between Penn and the abrupt rise of Bruston Hill."[1]

NOTE
> 1. John Edgar Wideman, Brothers and Keepers (New
> York: Penguin Books, 1984), 39.

1 Select endnotes or footnotes

Positioning footnotes between the body of the text and the bottom
margin can be quite difficult and time-consuming. For this reason, even
though it may be a bit easier for readers to look at the bottom of the page for
a note than to turn to the end of the paper, you should generally employ endnotes. Most readers mark the page containing the endnotes so they can refer
to notes with a minimum of disruption. Because readers may sometimes skip
consulting a note unless they are particularly interested in your sources, you
should make sure that you place all information necessary for understanding
your argument or explanation in the body of your paper and not in the notes.

2 Consider content and explanatory notes

At times you may wish to supplement your text with material that
may interest only a few readers. Notes are an appropriate place to do this,
but don't make notes so detailed that they distract readers from the main
text of the paper. You can also combine explanation with a source reference, though you need to make sure that a long and detailed discussion
does not obscure the reference.

TEXT OF PAPER   Another potential source of conflict, or at least misunderstanding, in the contemporary workplace comes from differences in the ways men commonly give orders (directly) and the ways women give orders (indirectly, often in the form of requests or questions).[2]

NOTE   2. Deborah Tannen, "How to Give Orders like a Man," New York Times Magazine, 18 August 1994, 46. It is sometimes easy to oversimplify the differences between the ways men and women use language. Tannen provides a detailed and balanced discussion in Talking from 9 to 5 (New York: William Morrow, 1994).

4b Creating CMS notes

After you have placed a number slightly above the line of text[3] to indicate the presence of an endnote or footnote and have made sure that your numbering system maintains consecutive order, you need to prepare the note. A typical note provides the author's name in regular order, the title of the work being cited, publication information, and the page number(s).

Place endnotes at the end of a paper, after appendixes but before a bibliography. Supply notes on a separate page with the centered heading "Notes." Indent the first line six spaces. Start the note with the number, followed by a period and a space. Do not indent the second line or any others that follow. Double-space for ease of reading.

Guide to CMS Formats for Notes

1. BOOKS AND WORKS TREATED AS BOOKS
1. One Author
2. Two or Three Authors
3. Four or More Authors
4. No Author Given
5. Editor
6. Edition Other than the First
7. Multivolume Work

2. ARTICLES AND SELECTIONS FROM BOOKS
8. Article in Journal Paginated by Volume
9. Article in Journal Paginated by Issue
10. Article in Popular Magazine
11. Article in Daily Newspaper
12. Chapter in Book or Selection from Anthology

3. FIELD RESOURCES
13. Unpublished Interview

4. MEDIA AND ELECTRONIC RESOURCES
14. Audio or Video Recording
15. Electronic Information Service
16. CD-ROM
17. Online Book
18. Online Article

5. MULTIPLE SOURCES AND SOURCES CITED IN PRIOR NOTES
19. Multiple Sources
20. Book or Article Cited More than Once

1 Books and works treated as books

MODEL FORMAT FOR BOOKS AND WORKS TREATED AS BOOKS

```
        note              comma
      number             + space    space
        ↓                   ↓         ↓
      1. Author(s), Title (Place of Publication:
Publisher, Year), Page number(s).
                          ↑
                      comma + space
```

- **Author(s).** Give the name of the author(s) in regular order followed by a comma and a space.
- **Title.** Give the title of the work being cited. Underline the title of a book and follow the title with a space. (Follow rules for capitalization in <u>The Longman Handbook for Readers and Writers</u>.)
- **Publication information.** Give all publication information within parentheses. Start with the city of publication, followed by a comma and an abbreviation for the state or country if this information is necessary to avoid confusion between two cities with the same name or to identify little-known places. Add a colon and a space; then give the publisher's name followed by a comma, a space, and the date of publication. Place a comma followed by a space after the closing parenthesis mark.
- **Page number(s).** Conclude with the specific page numbers containing the information being cited or the passage being quoted, paraphrased, or summarized.

1. One Author

> 1. Ruth Macklin, <u>Mortal Choices: Ethical Dilemmas in Modern Medicine</u> (Boston: Houghton Mifflin, 1987), 154.

2. Two or Three Authors

Separate the names of two authors with *and.* Separate those of three authors with commas as well as *and* before the name of the third author.

> 2. Mary Knapp and Herbert Knapp, <u>One Potato, Two Potato . . .: The Secret Education of American Children</u> (New York: W. W. Norton, 1978), 144.

> 2. Michael Wood, Bruce Cole, and Adelheid Gealt, <u>Art of the Western World</u> (New York: Summit Books, 1989), 206-10.

3. Four or More Authors

For works with more than three authors, give the name of the first author followed by *and others*. (Generally, all the names are supplied in the corresponding bibliography entry.)

3. Anthony Slide and others, <u>The American Film Industry: A Historical Dictionary</u> (New York: Greenwood Press, 1986), 124.

4. No Author Given

If the author is not known, begin the entry with the title.

4. <u>The Great Utopia: The Russian and Soviet Avant-Garde, 1915-1932</u> (New York: Guggenheim Museum, 1992), 661.

5. Editor

When a work has an editor, translator, or compiler (or some combination of these), give the name or names after the title preceded by a comma and the appropriate abbreviation, for example, *ed., trans.,* or *comp.*

5. Charles Dickens, <u>Bleak House</u>, ed. Norman Page (Harmondsworth, England: Penguin Books, 1971), 49.
Dickens is the author, and Page has prepared the particular edition of the work.

If you wish to emphasize the role of the editor, translator, or compiler, give his or her name at the beginning of the entry.

5. Donald M. Scott and Bernard Wishy, eds., <u>America's Families: A Documentary History</u> (New York: Harper & Row, 1982), 177.
The editors are responsible for assembling materials from a variety of sources.

5. Robert H. Ferrell, ed., <u>Dear Bess: The Letters from Harry to Bess Truman 1910-1959</u> (New York: W. W. Norton, 1983), 71-2.
The word *by* with the author's name (*Harry S. Truman*) would be appropriate following the title, but it is not necessary because the author's name appears in the title.

6. Edition Other than the First

Use an abbreviation following the title to indicate the particular edition, for example, *4th ed.* ("fourth edition") or *rev. and enl. ed.* ("revised and enlarged edition").

```
      6. John D. La Plante, Asian Art, 3d ed.
(Dubuque, Iowa: Wm. C. Brown, 1992), 7.
```

For a work that has been reprinted or appears in a special paperback edition, give information about both the original publication and the reprint.

```
      6. Henri Frankfort and others, The
Intellectual Adventure of Ancient Man (Chicago:
University of Chicago Press, 1946; reprint,
Chicago: University of Chicago Press, 1977),
202-4 (page citations are to the reprint
edition).
```

7. Multivolume Work

A multivolume work can consist of volumes all by a single author (sometimes with different titles for each) or of works by a variety of authors with an overall title. If you are referring to the whole multivolume work, include the number of volumes after the title. To indicate volume and page number for a specific volume, use volume and page numbers separated by a colon and no space. Give the volume number and name for separately titled volumes after the main title and omit the volume number in the page reference.

```
      7. Sigmund Freud, The Standard Edition of
the Complete Psychological Works of Sigmund
Freud, trans. James Strachey (London: Hogarth
Press, 1953), 11:180.
```

2 Articles and selections from books

MODEL FORMAT FOR ARTICLES AND SELECTIONS

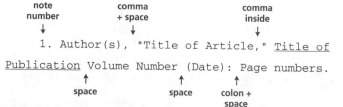

- **Author(s).** Give the author's name in regular order.
- **Title.** Put the title of the article or selection in quotation marks. Put a comma inside the closing quotation mark, and leave a space after the quotation mark.
- **Publication information.** Next give the title of the journal or book, underlined, and leave a space after it with no punctuation.

Supply the volume number and then the date of publication in parentheses, varying the information and style for different types of publications (see below). Place a colon after the final parenthesis, and leave a space.

• **Page number(s).** Supply the page numbers for the pertinent part of the article or selection.

8. Article in Journal Paginated by Volume

When the page numbers run continuously through the individual issues that make up a volume, give the volume number but do not include the month, season, or number of the individual issue containing the article. Give specific page numbers for the part of the article you are citing. If you wish to refer to the article as a whole, give inclusive page numbers for the entire article, for example, *98–114.*

> 8. C. Anita Tarr, "'A Man Can Stand Up': Johnny Tremain and the Rebel Pose," <u>The Lion and the Unicorn: A Critical Journal of Children's Literature</u> 18 (1994): 181.

9. Article in Journal Paginated by Issue

If each issue of a journal begins with page 1, give the volume number followed by a comma, the abbreviation *no.* (for "number"), and the issue number. If the issue is instead identified by month or season, include this information just before the year and within the same set of parentheses, for example (*Winter 1994*) or (*February 1996*). Give page numbers for the specific part of the article you are citing or inclusive page numbers for the entire article if you are referring to it as a whole.

> 9. Peter Smagorinsky and Pamela K. Fly, "A New Perspective on Why Small Groups Do and Don't Work," <u>English Journal</u> 83, no. 5 (1994): 54–55.

10. Article in Popular Magazine

Follow the name of the magazine with a comma and the date. Use this order for the date if it includes the day: *25 November 1995.* Place a comma at the end of the date before the page number, and give a page number for the specific part of the article you are citing or inclusive page numbers for the entire article if you are referring to it as a whole.

> 10. Deborah Tannen, "But What Do You Mean?" <u>Redbook</u>, October 1994, 57–58.

11. Article in Daily Newspaper

Identify newspaper articles by date (rather than volume number) following the title of the article and the name of the newspaper. Present the date in this order: *4 February 1996.* When the sections of a newspaper are separately paginated, provide the section number or letter and the page number—for example, *sec. B, p. 3*—using *p.* or *pp.* to introduce the page number(s).

> 11. Debra West, "Stalking Weeds of Spring for Traditional Meals," <u>New York Times</u>, 18 May 1995, sec. B, pp. 1, 7.

When an American newspaper's title does not include the city's name, give it at the start of the title (underlined). For less known newspapers, for those outside North America with the city not mentioned in the title, and for those from places easily confused with well-known cities, give the name of the state or country after the title or after the name of the city in the title: *Westerly (R.I.) Sun; Times (London).*

12. Chapter in Book or Selection from Anthology

For a selection from an anthology or for a book chapter, give the name of the selection or chapter in quotation marks followed by *in* and the name of book. If the book has an editor, follow the book's title with *ed.* and the editor's name.

> 12. Fred Pfeil, "'Makin' Flippy-Floppy': Postmodernism and the Baby-Boom PMC," in <u>Another Tale to Tell: Politics and Narrative in Postmodern Culture</u> (London: Verso, 1990), 107.
>
> Chapter in a book.

> 12. W. E. B. Du Bois, "The Call of Kansas," in <u>W. E. B. Du Bois: A Reader</u>, ed. David Levering Lewis (New York: Henry Holt, 1995), 173.
>
> Selection from an edited collection of one writer's works.

> 12. Julie D'Acci, "Defining Women: The Case of Cagney and Lacey," in <u>Private Screenings: Television and the Female Consumer</u>, ed. Lynn Spigel and Denise Mann (Minneapolis: University of Minnesota Press, 1992), 169.
>
> Chapter in an edited collection of essays.

3 Field resources

13. Unpublished Interview

For unpublished interviews done by someone else, begin with the name of the person interviewed followed by a comma; then give the phrase *interview by,* the name of the interviewer, the date (in this order: *2 May 1978*), any file number, the medium (*tape recording* or *transcript,* for example), and the place where the interview is stored (such as *Erie County Historical Society, Buffalo, New York*). For interviews you conduct, provide the name of the person interviewed, the phrase *interview by author,* a description of the kind of interview, the medium, and the place and date of the interview.

> 13. Shawon Kelley, interview by author, tape recording, Los Angeles, Calif., 2 May 1995.
>
> 13. Morton Kosko, telephone interview by author, transcript, Scottsdale, Ariz., 22 January 1996.

4 Media and electronic resources

14. Audio or Video Recording

Start with the work's title unless the recording features a particular performer, composer, director, or writer. Give names and roles (if appropriate) of performers or others whose participation needs to be noted. Indicate the length of the recording (video), the company responsible, the recording number (audio), the date, and the medium (for example, *audiocassette* or *videocassette*).

> 14. <u>James Baldwin</u>, prod. and dir. Karen Thorsen, 87 min., Resolution Inc./California Newsreel, 1990, videocassette.

15. Electronic Information Service

For information and text you gather through an electronic information service, use whatever format would be appropriate for similar material available in printed form, but at the end of the entry provide the name of the service (such as *Dialog* or *ERIC*), the name of the vendor, and the accession or identifying numbers used by the service.

> 15. Mark Miller, "Two Beaked Whales Wash Up on Beach," <u>Daytona Beach News-Journal,</u> 20 January 1994, in Newsbank [database online] [cited 5 March 1995], ENV 3, G6.

16. CD-ROM

Supply information as you would for the print equivalent if it existed. After the title, indicate in brackets the type of medium: *[CD-ROM]*.

> 16. William Shakespeare, <u>All's Well That</u>
> <u>Ends Well. William Shakespeare: The Complete</u>
> <u>Works on CD-ROM</u> [CD-ROM] (Abingdon, England:
> Andromeda Interactive, 1994).

17. Online Book

For a book that has been previously published in print, include all information as required by Entries 1–7. Indicate the medium of the source in brackets following the title: *[book online]*. With the original publication date, give the date you accessed the source. Finally, indicate the URL at which the book is available and the network in brackets: *[Internet]*.

> 17. Charles Darwin, <u>On the Origin of</u>
> <u>Species by Means of Natural Selection, or the</u>
> <u>Preservation of Favoured Races in the Struggle</u>
> <u>for Life</u> [book online] (London: Down, Bromley,
> Kent, 1859 [cited 12 February 1999]); available
> from ftp://sailor.gutenberg.org/pub/gutenberg/
> etext98/otoos10.txt; [Internet].

18. Online Article

Include all information required in Entries 8 and 9. Following the publication information, indicate the medium of the source in brackets: *[journal online]*. Indicate the URL at which the book is available and the network in brackets: *[Internet]*. Include the date you accessed the source.

> 18. Aaron Lynch, "Units, Events and
> Dynamics in Memetic Evolution," <u>Journal of</u>
> <u>Memetics--Evolutionary Models of Information</u>
> <u>Transmission</u> 2.1, June 1998 [journal online]
> [cited 12 February 1999]; available from
> http://www.cpm.mmu.ac.uk/jom-emit/1998/vol2/
> lynch_a.html; [Internet].

5 Multiple sources and sources cited in prior notes

19. Multiple Sources

When you wish to cite more than one source in a note, separate the references with semicolons and give the entries in the order in which they were cited in the text.

```
     19. See Greil Marcus, Mystery Train:
Images of America in Rock 'n Roll Music
(New York: E. P. Dutton, 1975), 119; Susan
Orlean, "All Mixed Up," New Yorker, 22 June
1992, 90; and Cornel West, "Learning to Talk
of Race," New York Times Magazine, 2 August
1992, 24.
```

20. Book or Article Cited More than Once

The first time you provide a reference to a work, you need to list full information about the source in the note. In later notes you need to provide only the last name of the author(s), a shortened title, and the page(s). Separate these elements with commas.

```
     21. Macklin, Mortal, 161.
     21. Wood, Cole, and Gealt, Art, 207.
```

If a note refers to the same source as the note before, you can use a traditional scholarly abbreviation, *ibid.* (from the Latin for "in the same place"), for the second note. *Ibid.* means that the entire reference is identical, but if you add a new page reference, the addition shows that the specific page is different.

```
     22. Tarr, "'A Man,'" 183.
     23. Ibid.
     24. Ibid., 186.
```

4c Creating a CMS bibliography

At the end of your paper you need to provide readers with an alphabetical list of the sources cited in your notes. CMS style calls for this list to be titled "Selected Bibliography" or "Sources Consulted" if it includes all the works you consulted. If you want to limit the list to the works appearing in your notes, you might call it "Works Cited," "References," or a similar title.

Place your bibliography on a separate page at the end of your paper, and center the title two inches below the upper edge. Continue the page numbering used for the text. Double-space entries for ease of reading. Do not indent the first line, but indent the second line and any subsequent lines five spaces. Alphabetize the entries according to the authors' last names or the first word of the title, excluding *A, An,* and *The*, if the author is unknown.

Guide to CMS Formats for Bibliography Entries

1. BOOKS AND WORKS TREATED AS BOOKS

1. One Author
2. Two or Three Authors
3. Four or More Authors
4. No Author Given
5. Editor
6. Edition Other than the First
7. Multivolume Work

2. ARTICLES AND SELECTIONS FROM BOOKS

8. Article in Journal Paginated by Volume
9. Article in Journal Paginated by Issue
10. Article in Popular Magazine
11. Article in Daily Newspaper
12. Chapter in Book or Selection from Anthology

3. OTHER PRINTED AND FIELD RESOURCES

13. Unpublished Interview

4. MEDIA AND ELECTRONIC RESOURCES

14. Audio or Video Recording
15. Electronic Information Service
16. CD-ROM
17. Online Book
18. Online Article

5. MULTIPLE SOURCES

19. Multiple Sources

---

1 Books and works treated as books

MODEL FORMAT FOR BOOKS AND WORKS TREATED AS BOOKS

```
        period +   period +              colon +
         space      space                 space
           ↓          ↓                     ↓
Author(s).  Title.  Place of Publication:
     Publisher,  Date.
   ↑              ↑
 indent     comma + space
 5 spaces
```

- **Author(s).** Give the author's last name followed by a comma, then the first and any middle names or initials followed by a period and a space.
- **Title.** Give the title of the work, underlined, ending with a period and space. Capitalize the main words of the title and any subtitle. Do not capitalize *a, an, the,* coordinating conjunctions (such as *and, or,* and *but*), and prepositions. Always capitalize the first and last words of any title or subtitle.
- **Place of publication.** Give the city where the work was published, followed by a comma and an abbreviation for the state or country if necessary to avoid confusion between cities with the same name or to identify little-known places. End with a colon and a space.

- **Publisher.** Give the publisher's name followed by a comma and a single space.
- **Date.** Give the date of publication followed by a period.

1. One Author

Macklin, Ruth. <u>Mortal Choices: Ethical Dilemmas in Modern Medicine</u>. Boston: Houghton Mifflin, 1987.

2. Two or Three Authors

Knapp, Mary, and Herbert Knapp. <u>One Potato, Two Potato . . .: The Secret Education of American Children</u>. New York: W. W. Norton, 1978.

Wood, Michael, Bruce Cole, and Adelheid Gealt. <u>Art of the Western World</u>. New York: Summit Books, 1989.

3. Four or More Authors

Slide, Anthony, Val Almen Darez, Robert Gitt, and Susan Perez Prichard. <u>The American Film Industry: A Historical Dictionary</u>. New York: Greenwood Press, 1986.

4. No Author Given

<u>The Great Utopia: The Russian and Soviet Avant-Garde, 1915-1932</u>. New York: Guggenheim Museum, 1992.

5. Editor

Dickens, Charles. <u>Bleak House</u>. Edited by Norman Page. Harmondsworth, England: Penguin Books, 1971.

Ferrell, Robert H., ed. <u>Dear Bess: The Letters from Harry to Bess Truman 1910-1959</u>. New York: W. W. Norton, 1983.

Scott, Donald M., and Bernard Wishy, eds. <u>America's Families: A Documentary History</u>. New York: Harper & Row, 1982.

6. Edition Other than the First

```
Frankfort, Henri, H. A. Frankfort, John A.
     Wilson, Thorkild Jacobsen, and William A.
     Irving. The Intellectual Adventure of
     Ancient Man. Chicago: University of
     Chicago Press, 1946. Reprint, Chicago:
     University of Chicago Press, 1977.
La Plante, John D. Asian Art. 3d ed. Dubuque,
     Iowa: Wm. C. Brown, 1992.
```

7. Multivolume Work

```
Freud, Sigmund. The Standard Edition of the
     Complete Psychological Works of Sigmund
     Freud. Translated by James Strachey. Vol.
     11. London: Hogarth Press, 1953.
```

2   Articles and selections from books

MODEL FORMAT FOR ARTICLES AND SELECTIONS FROM BOOKS

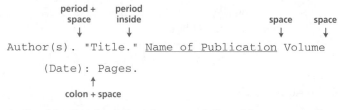

- **Author(s).** Give the author's last name followed by a comma, then the first and any middle names or initials followed by a period and a space.
- **Title.** Give the title of the article within quotation marks, and capitalize the main words of the title and of any subtitle. Do not capitalize *a, an, the,* coordinating conjunctions (such as *and* and *or*), and prepositions. Always capitalize the first and last words of any title or subtitle. If the article's title contains the title of a work that needs to be italicized or underlined, use underlining; if it contains a title that requires quotation marks, use single quotation marks to enclose the interior title.
- **Name of publication.** Give the title of the journal or magazine containing the article, and underline it.
- **Volume.** Give the volume number of the periodical; separate it from the name of the publication by a space without a comma or any other punctuation. Include the issue number only for certain kinds of publications.

- **Date.** Provide the year in which the article was published (within parentheses), but indicate the month or season only for certain kinds of publications.
- **Pages.** Follow the parentheses containing the date with a colon and a space; then give the inclusive pages on which the article appears.

8. Article in Journal Paginated by Volume

Tarr, Anita C. "'A Man Can Stand Up': Johnny Tremain and the Rebel Pose." <u>The Lion and the Unicorn: A Critical Journal of Children's Literature</u> 18 (1994): 178-189.

9. Article in Journal Paginated by Issue

Smagorinsky, Peter, and Pamela K. Fly. "A New Perspective on Why Small Groups Do and Don't Work." <u>English Journal</u> 83, no. 5 (1994): 54-58.

10. Article in Popular Magazine

Tannen, Deborah. "But What Do You Mean?" <u>Redbook</u>, October 1994, 57-58.

11. Article in Daily Newspaper

West, Debra. "Stalking Weeds of Spring for Traditional Meals." <u>New York Times</u>, 18 May 1995, sec. B, pp. 1, 7.

12. Chapter in Book or Selection from Anthology

D'Acci, Julie. "Defining Women: The Case of Cagney and Lacey." In <u>Private Screenings: Television and the Female Consumer</u>, edited by Lynn Spigel and Denise Mann, 169-201. Minneapolis: University of Minnesota Press, 1992.

Du Bois, W. E. B. "The Call of Kansas." <u>In W. E. B. Du Bois: A Reader</u>, edited by David Levering Lewis, 101-121. New York: Henry Holt, 1995.

```
Pfeil, Fred. "'Makin' Flippy-Floppy':
     Postmodernism and the Baby-Boom PMC."
     Chap. in Another Tale to Tell: Politics
     and Narrative in Postmodern Culture.
     London: Verso, 1990.
```

3 Other printed and field resources
13. Unpublished Interview

```
Kelley, Shawon. Interview by author. Tape
     recording. Los Angeles, Calif., 2 May 1995.
Kosko, Morton. Telephone interview by the
     author. Transcript. Scottsdale, Ariz., 22
     January 1996.
```

4 Media and electronic resources
14. Audio or Video Recording

```
James Baldwin. Produced and directed by Karen
     Thorsen. 87 min. Resolution
     Inc./California Newsreel, 1990.
     Videocassette.
```

15. Electronic Information Service

```
Miller, Mark. "Two Beaked Whales Wash Up on
     Beach." Daytona Beach News-Journal, 20
     January 1994. Database online. Available
     from Newsbank, ENV 3, G6.
```

16. CD-ROM

```
Shakespeare, William. All's Well That Ends
     Well. William Shakespeare: The Complete
     Works on CD-ROM [CD-ROM]. Abingdon,
     England: Andromeda Interactive, 1994.
```

17. Online Book

```
Darwin, Charles. On the Origin of Species by
     Means of Natural Selection, or the
     Preservation of Favoured Races in the
```

<u>Struggle for Life</u> [book online]. London: Down, Bromley, Kent, 1859 [cited 12 February 1999]. Available from ftp://sailor.gutenberg.org/pub/gutenberg/ etext98/otoos10.txt; [Internet].

18. Online Article

Lynch, Aaron. "Units, Events and Dynamics in Memetic Evolution." <u>Journal of Memetics-- Evolutionary Models of Information Transmission</u> 2.1, June 1998 [journal online] [cited 12 February 1999]. Available from http://www.cpm.mmu.ac.uk/ jom-emit/1998/vol2/lynch_a.html; [Internet].

5 Multiple sources

19. Multiple Sources

When a note lists more than one source, list each one separately in your bibliography, presenting them in alphabetical order among your other sources.

Exercise

 A. Turn to Exercise A in Chapter 49. Rewrite the sentences supplied there to add note numbers in CMS style. Then prepare the corresponding notes for these items.

 B. Turn to Exercise B in Chapter 49. Rewrite the items supplied there to create a list of works cited in CMS style.

 C. Working with a partner or a small group, compare your answers to Exercises A and B above. Correct any errors in your answers, using your handbook or your instructor's advice to resolve any differences of opinion.

5

Documenting Sources: COS

Written in collaboration with Margaret M. Barber, University of Southern Colorado, and Janice R. Walker, Georgia Southern University

The World Wide Web (WWW) and Internet are quickly expanding as digital storehouses of books and articles previously available only on paper. Electronic databases and search engines allow researchers to locate sources to read onscreen or print out and read at leisure.

Electronic publication also permits new modes of authoring and creation of new kinds of text in which documentation styles developed for traditional materials are difficult to apply. Key ingredients needed for citations in MLA, APA, CMS, and CBE styles, such as names of authors, publication dates, and page numbers, may be missing from online texts; electronic addresses, critical for locating online sources, do not appear in traditional citation formats.

Columbia Online Style (COS) was developed by Janice R. Walker and Todd Taylor to respond to the need for ways to cite electronic sources in formats consistent with MLA, APA, CMS, CBE, or other traditional styles. Designed to be used in combination with one of these other styles, COS provides an efficient and flexible model for writers to adapt for citing materials found online.

If you have any doubt about what documentation style to use for electronic sources, find out what your instructor requires. The indexes in 5d and 5f cover the most common kinds of online sources. For other sources, see *The Columbia Guide to Online Style* by Janice R. Walker and Todd Taylor, published by Columbia University Press (1998) and updated on the Web at http://www.columbia.edu/cu/cup/cgos/.

USE **COS** FOR DOCUMENTATION OF ELECTRONIC SOURCES IN . . .

ACADEMIC SETTINGS

> When you are already using MLA, CMS, APA, or CBE documentation style
>
> When an instructor or editor does not specify another documentation style for online sources

WORK AND PUBLIC SETTINGS

> For written memos or reports in which you use ideas or language from online sources, including email
>
> When you can gain credibility by using authoritative sources found online, such as a letter to a newspaper editor

5a How to use COS for documentation

Before composing a rough draft, determine which documentation style you will be using in your paper—either MLA or CMS in the humanities or APA or CBE in the sciences—and study the chapter in this book that fully explains that style. Follow the chapter's guidelines for determining what to document, what not to document, when to use parenthetical citations, and when to use endnotes or footnotes.

Use two steps to document an electronic source with COS, just as you would with MLA, APA, or another style for print sources. First, place parenthetical citations at appropriate places within the text according to the style you are using in your paper, following the directions in 5b. Then, when you have finished the first draft, make a list of every source referred to in a parenthetical citation. Use this list to compile a list of citations (called a list of works cited in the humanities or a reference list in the sciences) following the directions in the chapter you are using for documenting print sources.

For material found online, study the basic format for citations in 5c. Then refer to the indexes in 5d (MLA/humanities) and 5f (APA/sciences) to locate the kind of electronic source you are citing. Use the numbered key to find instructions for devising each kind of citation. Your citation should conform to the example in terms of spacing, punctuation, use of capital and lowercase letters, italics, and parentheses. Combine your finished citations of print sources with those of online sources in one works cited or reference list, alphabetized by author, title, or other item that appears first in each citation.

5b Creating in-text citations

For MLA style, the typical citation for print sources will contain, in parentheses, the author's surname and the page number where the material used was found: (*Wiseman 9*). When using COS in the humanities, however, omit the page numbers in parenthetical citations unless they are provided in the electronic version. You will often find that online texts do not share the page-numbering conventions of print materials.

MLA IN-TEXT CITATION

A writing teacher explores an important lesson learned from baseball in his essay on teaching writing to a student who finds a way to "blend failure with hope and learning" (Hochman).

You may omit the parenthetical citation entirely if you work the author's name into the text.

AUTHOR'S NAME AS PART OF DISCUSSION

Will Hochman explores an important lesson learned from baseball in his essay on teaching writing to a student who finds a way to "blend failure with hope and learning."

GENERAL REFERENCE

Use only one citation at the end of a paragraph containing consecutive references to the same online source when no page numbers appear in parenthetical citations to indicate that different portions of the source were used. For material from several sources interspersed throughout a paragraph, indicate authorship for some sources in the text proper, where practicable, to minimize the need for parenthetical citations.

APA style in-text citations for print material includes the name, the date, and, when reference is to a specific passage, a page number or numbers.

APA IN-TEXT CITATION

(Jacobson, 1989, p. 22)

COS/scientific and CMS author-date styles use the same format as APA style, placing the author's last name and the date of publication in the citation.

COS/SCIENTIFIC IN-TEXT CITATION

(Hochman, 1998)

If you work the author's name into the text, the parenthetical reference needs to include only the date.

Will Hochman (1998) explores an important lesson learned from baseball in his essay on teaching writing.

NO AUTHOR GIVEN

In COS/humanities style, if the author's name is missing, use a shortened version of the title instead, placing the title in quotation marks, just as you would for print sources.

("Social Statistics")

For COS/scientific style, use the shortened version of the title, without quotation marks, and include the date of publication. If no publication date is indicated in an electronic source, provide the date of access, including the day, the month (abbreviated except for May, June, or July), and the year.

(Social statistics, 19 Dec. 1998)

If the electronic source uses only a nickname or an alias for an author's name, use the alias in your parenthetical citation. In COS/humanities style, just as with MLA style, if the author's name or alias is worked into your text, no parenthetical reference is needed. In COS/scientific style, however, a date of publication or access is placed in a parenthetical citation.

Vanessa, a new visitor to the Spanish language MOO, *Mundo Hispanico,* found that other students gently suggested word choices until they could understand her meaning (19 Dec. 1998).

If you use CMS for documentation, your endnotes or footnotes for online sources will include the distinctive elements in the works cited entries described below. Check with your instructor to determine whether or not to include a separate list of references, which is optional in different forms of CMS style. To create endnotes or footnotes for use with CMS style, find the section in the form index in 4c, that corresponds with the type of electronic source you are citing. Follow COS guidelines, making any adjustments necessary to meet the basic requirements of CMS style.

5c Creating an entry for a works cited or reference list

Citations in humanities and scientific styles for print and online sources have key elements in common. Information on authorship, the titles of documents and complete works, names of publishers, and places and dates of publication allow a reader to determine the extent and quality of the author's research. Above all, such information permits the reader to identify and locate the original source. Major components of print and online materials, however, differ in some important ways that require variations in citation form.

- **Author.** Some online articles and Web sites have individually named authors. Others are designed by unidentified Webmasters or development teams working for organizations or corporations. Sites may be "compiled" or "maintained" by individuals who write some of the materials that appear but also organize material submitted by others and create links to documents housed at other sites. Using pseudonyms, a group of writers in the same room or building may create a single document by writing on computers connected by a local area network (LAN). Fiction writers using aliases may co-author stories by writing "synchronously" (at the same time) on MOOs. Others using made-up log-in names may join a newsgroup to discuss their common interest in a hobby or sport. Colleagues scattered around the globe in different time zones, usually using their own names, form email lists to discuss professional concerns in "asynchronous" conferences, reading and writing at different times that suit their convenience. Variations on ways to author online documents continue to proliferate.

For a citation using COS, list an individual, institutional, or corporate author if you can find one named. This information is often located at the bottom of the home page of a Web site. Cite an alias or log-in name if that is all you can find. Otherwise, refer to the examples in 5d or 5f for instructions on devising citations for sources without named authors.

- **Title.** The title of a document, such as an article, a poem, an essay, or a single Web page, appears after the individual or group author's name or, if no author is named, as the first item in the citation. The title of the complete work, such as an online journal or Web site, follows in italics. Italicize all titles of complete works when using COS. Use italics instead of underlining in the works cited or reference list to avoid confusion with uses of underlining specific to online publication, particularly the designation of hypertext links.

- **Publication information.** Citations for works previously published in print should contain the original publication information (city, publisher, year) followed by online publication information, including the title of the site where the document is stored; a file name or number, if applicable; the date of publication; and the electronic address, with path or directory names if there are any.

- **Electronic address.** The electronic address or URL (for uniform resource locator) is the single most essential piece of information for locating materials online. It must always be given in full and with precision, down to the last period or "dot." It begins with a protocol such as *http* (HyperText Transfer Protocol), *ftp* (file transfer protocol), *gopher,* or *telnet* in lowercase letters, followed by the main part of the address. In files accessed by using a Web browser, the address usually consists of the protocol with a colon and two slashes (for example, *gopher://*), a domain name (a unique identifier for an Internet host computer), any paths or directories needed to locate the material, and the file name. Do not use angle brackets around the electronic address or add punctuation at the end. Follow the URL with a single space and the opening parenthesis for the date of access.

- **Dates of publication and access.** An online document such as a Web page may be published without any indication of the date, or it may be revised periodically, even hourly, making a single date of publication impossible to determine. Provide the date of original publication, if available. COS follows the conventions of MLA and APA styles for providing dates. In addition, a date of last revision is included, if known.

The last term in the citation is the date of access, placed immediately after the electronic address and a single space. The date of access is always enclosed in parentheses. Include the day, month (abbreviated except for May, June, and July), and year you visited the site. Follow the closing parenthesis with a period, as in

http://www.uscolo.edu (20 Dec. 1998).

The date of access indicates exactly when you visited the site. It is important because online sources are subject to change. When the date of publication and the date of access are identical, as with frequently updated sites, omit the date of publication. When the publication date is unknown, or when the date of revision is the same as the date of access, use the date of access instead. The date of access is never omitted.

5d Using COS in the humanities (with MLA, CMS)

The basic format for citing online sources in a works cited list is as follows.

```
Author's Surname, First Name. "Title of

    Document." Title of Complete Work. File or

    version number. Date of document or date

    of last revision. Protocol and address,

    access path, or directories (Date of

    access).
```

List the individual author of the site, last name first, followed by a comma, the first name or initial (whichever is required by the style you are using for print citations), a period, and a space. The title of the document or article, in quotation marks, is followed by a period placed inside the closing quotation mark. Capitalize words in the title as you would in an MLA or CMS entry. Give the title of a complete work such as an online journal or book, a site that organizes contributions by multiple authors, or a site that links together other sites (such as the *Virtual Jerusalem* "supersite" at http://www.virtualjerusalem.com). Follow with a period. Provide file or version numbers, if applicable.

Give the date the document was first published or, if available, the date of last revision, followed by a period. Omit these dates if they are identical to the date of access. Give the complete electronic address, including any path names or directories. Follow with a single space, the date of access in parentheses, and a period. If you cannot find one or more of these items, omit them, but always include an electronic address and date of access.

Brown, Mitchell C. "The Past: What Has Happened
　　　Before." *The Faces of Science: African*
　　　Americans in the Sciences. Rev. 31 Aug.
　　　1998. http://www.lib.lsu.edu/lib/
　　　chem/display/faces.html#Past (28 Dec. 1998).

Guide to COS/Humanities Formats for a List of Works Cited

1. Citations from the World Wide Web (WWW)
1. WWW Site
2. WWW Site—Revised, Updated, or Modified
3. WWW Site—Authored by Group, Organization, or Institution
4. WWW Site—Corporate Author
5. WWW Site—Without Named Author, Group, or Title
6. WWW Site—Maintained or Compiled by Individual
7. WWW Site—Government
8. WWW Site—Printed Book Available Online
9. WWW Site—Electronic Book
10. WWW Site—Online Article
11. WWW Site—Article from News Service or Online Newspaper
12. WWW Site—Article from Archive (Previously Published in Print)
13. WWW Site—With Frames
14. WWW Site—Graphic or Audio File

2. Email Messages, Discussion Lists, or Newsgroups
15. Email—Personal
16. Email—Discussion List
17. Email—From Newsgroup
18. Email—From Message Archive

3. Materials Obtained via Gopher, FTP, or Telnet
19. Via Gopher or FTP
20. Via Telnet

4. Synchronous Conference Records
21. MOOs, MUDs
22. LANs

5. Reference Tools and Databases
23. Entry in Online Dictionary
24. Article in Online Encyclopedia
25. Information on CD-ROM
26. Article from Online Database

6. Software
27. Software/Video Game

1 Citations from the World Wide Web
1. WWW Site

```
Hochman, Will. "Beyond Exception: The Writer's

     Life." The Salt River Review 1.1 (1998).

     http://www.mc.maricopa.edu/users/cervantes/

     SRR/hochman.html (20 Dec. 1998).
```

2. WWW Site—Revised, Updated, or Modified

Before the electronic address, indicate the date the site was revised or modified, preceded by *Rev.* for "Revised" or *Mod.* for "Modified," depending on the terminology used on the page itself. Look for revision information in a side column or near the bottom of the page. Use the numeral for the day and an abbreviation for the month (unless it is May, June, or July), and give the year followed by a period. List the address and date of access.

```
AFL-CIO. "Facts About Working Women." Today's

     Unions. Rev. 7 Dec. 1998. http://www.aflcio.org/

     women/wwfacts.htm (19 Dec. 1998).
```

3. WWW Site—Authored by Group, Organization, or Institution

If a group, organization, or institution sponsors a site and no individual author is named, use the name of the group in place of the author.

```
International Olympic Committee. "Welcome to

     the Official Site of the International

     Olympic Committee." The Official Site of

     the International Olympic Committee.

     http://www.olympic.org (27 Dec. 1998).
```

4. WWW Site—Corporate Author

When a corporation serves as the author of a page, use its full name, and then give the page's title in quotation marks.

```
Goodwill Industries International, Inc.

     "Goodwill Career Links." Rev. 18 Dec. 1998.
```

```
http://www.goodwill.org/about/careerlk.htm
(19 Dec. 1998).
```

If the complete site has a title different from the name of the corporation used as author, place it after the title of the individual page, in italics.

```
LatinoLink Enterprises, Inc. "Job Bank."
     LatinoLink. 1998. http://www.latinolink .com/
     joblist.html (29 Dec. 1998).
```

5. WWW Site—Without Named Author, Group, or Title

When an author or authoring group is unnamed on a page, begin with the title in quotation marks or italics and follow with the Web address and date accessed.

```
"Social Statistics Briefing Room."
     http://www.whitehouse.gov/fsbr/ssbr.html
     (19 Dec. 1998).
```

If both author and title are omitted, begin with the file name.

```
chorusline.mpg. http://www.juggling.org/
     animations/chorusline.mpg (20 Dec. 1998).
```

6. WWW Site—Maintained or Compiled by Individual

A maintained site is one in which a Web designer organizes and posts information gathered from several sources, often including members of a sponsoring organization, much as a newsletter editor would do. The maintainer may also provide an index to material on other sites. For a maintained site, give the site's title first, and then the name of the maintainer, preceded by the abbreviation *maint.* For the author of a compiled site, one that consists primarily of links to other sites, use *comp.* for "compiler."

```
Southeast Colorado RC&D, Inc. Colorado
     Southeast Network. Comp. Alex Bray.
     http://www.ruralnet.net/~csn (17 Dec.
     1998).
```

If your reference is specifically to the work of the maintainer or compiler, give that name first, followed by *maint.* or *comp.*

```
Freeland, Cynthia, maint. SWIP—The Society for
     Women in Philosophy. Jan. 1997. http://
     www .uh.edu/~cfreelan/SWIP/ (17 Dec. 1998).
```

If the maintainer or compiler is not named, simply omit that information.

```
"Computers and Academic Freedom." Academic
     Freedom Policy Statements Archive. http://
     www.eff.org/pub/CAF/academic (27 Dec.
     1998).
```

7. WWW Site—Government

Use the name of the sponsoring government agency in place of the author. Note that for a site that is updated every few minutes, the date of publication is identical to the date of access.

```
U.S. Census Bureau. "POPClocks." U.S. Census
     Bureau: The Official Statistics.
     http://www.census.gov/main/www/popclock
     .html (27 Dec. 1998).
```

8. WWW Site—Printed Book Available Online

Many books first published on paper are now available online. To cite the online version, give the original print publication information, where available, followed by the electronic publication information, including the URL and date accessed. According to MLA style, when a book is published under a pseudonym, the author's real name is placed in brackets. If you know the name of the editor of the hypertext version, place it just before the Web address.

```
Twain, Mark [Samuel Langhorne Clemens]. Innocents
     Abroad: or, The New Pilgrim's Progress.
     Hartford: American, 1869. http://etext
     .virginia.edu/railton/innocent/iahompag
     .html (18 Dec. 1998).
```

9. WWW Site—Electronic Book

Electronic "books" might be more accurately described as hypertext narratives or interactive narratives. A site may have a single author using his or her real name or multiple authors using pseudonyms and writing simultaneously at a MOO or contributing asynchronously to a developing text. Give the primary author's name, if known; the title of the work in italics; the date of publication or last revision; the electronic address; and the date of access.

> *The Company Therapist*. 1996. Rev. 19 Dec. 1998.
>
> http://www.thetherapist.com/index.html
>
> (21 Dec. 1998).

10. WWW Site—Online Article

List the author(s), followed by the article title in quotation marks and the usual publication information. Include the volume and issue numbers, if applicable, separated by a period. If both are included, place the date of publication in parentheses.

> Palmquist, Mike, Will Hochman, Beth Kolko,
>
> Emily Golson, Jonathan Alexander, Luann
>
> Barnes, and Kate Kiefer. "Hypertext
>
> Reflections: Exploring the Rhetoric,
>
> Poetics, and Pragmatics of Hypertext."
>
> *Kairos* 2.2 (1997). http://english.ttu.edu/
>
> kairos/2.2/features/reflections/bridge
>
> .html (16 Dec. 1998).

11. WWW Site—Article from News Service or Online Newspaper

Give the name of the author, if known, or the name of the news source (for example, *Associated Press*); the title of the article in quotation marks; the title of the news service or online newspaper in italics; and other information as usual. When the date of publication is the same as the date of access, use only the latter.

> Espy, David. "House Votes To Impeach Clinton."
>
> *Yahoo! News*. http://dailynews.yahoo.com/
>
> headlines/ap/washington/story.html?s+v/ap/
>
> 19981219/pl/ (19 Dec. 1998).

12. WWW Site—Article from Archive (Previously Published in Print)

Give the author's name; the title of the article in quotation marks; the name of the journal in italics; the volume and issue numbers, if applicable; and the date of publication. List the name of the archive in italics, followed by the electronic address and the date accessed.

> Hauben, Michael F. "The Netizens and Community
>
> Networks." *Computer Mediated Communication*
>
> *Magazine* 4.2 (1997). *CMC Magazine Archive.*
>
> http://www.december.com/cmc/mag/1997/feb/
>
> hauben.html (16 Dec. 1998).

13. WWW Site—With Frames

For a document without its own URL, provide the italicized title of the page from which it was linked, the date of publication, and the electronic address of the main page, followed by a single blank space and the link(s) needed to reach the document.

> "Studies of Intermarriage Underway."
>
> *Communities in Transition* 1.1 (1995).
>
> http://www.hebrewcollege.edu/wilstein/
>
> index.html Wilstein Institute News (17
>
> Dec. 1998).

14. WWW Site—Graphic or Audio File

To cite a graphic or audio file alone, list the artist, photographer, or composer first; the title of the work, in italics if the work was first published separately, in quotation marks if it was first published as part of a larger work; the date it was produced; the address; and the date of access. To refer to the item within the context of a Web page, add the title of the page before the Web address.

> Seares, Robert. *Einstein with Young People.* 26
>
> Feb. 1931. "PhotoNet." *California*
>
> *Institute of Technology: Institute*
>
> *Archives.* http://www.caltech.edu/
>
> cgi-bin/arctohtml?1.8.1-12 (20 Dec. 1998).

2 Email messages, discussion lists, or newsgroups

15. Email—Personal

Always ask permission to cite a personal email message. Give the sender's real or log-in name and omit the email address. Use the subject line, in quotation marks, in place of a title; indicate that the message is personal email and follow with the date of the message.

```
Osborne, Paula. "Family Reunion." Personal
    email (19 Dec. 1998).
```

16. Email—Discussion List

Use the format for personal email, adding the name of the discussion list in italics between the date of the message and the address of the list. Unless the message has been retrieved from an archive, the date the message was sent serves as the date of access. Obtain permission from the sender to quote or use an email message in your work.

```
Kemp, Fred. "Digital Learning Communities."
    RHETNET. RHETNET-L@MIZZOU1.missouri.edu (4
    Sep. 1996).
```

17. Email—From Newsgroups

List the author's name or alias, the message's subject line in quotation marks, and its date if other than the date of access; give the name of the newsgroup in italics (if applicable), the newsgroup's protocol and address, and the date accessed.

```
Maffetone, Phil. "Re: Running and Carbohydrate
    Diet." 13 Dec. 1998. news:rec.running. (22
    Mar. 1999).
```

18. Email—From Message Archive

Give the author's real name or log-in name, the subject line of the message in quotation marks, the date of the post, the title of the discussion list (if known) in italics, and the list address. Then list the name of the archive in italics, the archive address of the post, and the date of access.

```
Caraveo, Shane. "New Stuff at NativeWeb." 20
    Aug. 1998. News, Announcements, and
    Information List. nw-news@nativeweb.org.
    Wotanging Ikche: Native American News
    Archives. http://www.nativeWeb.org/
    archives/news/9808/msg00000.html
    (21 Dec. 1998).
```

3 Materials obtained via gopher, ftp, or telnet

19. Via Gopher or FTP

Give the author's name, the title of the work, and original publication information if the work was previously published in print, including the city, publisher, and date. Then give complete information about the electronic version, including its title in quotation marks, any file or version numbers, the date of electronic publication or last revision, the title of database (if applicable) in italics, the protocol and address with any paths or directories, and the date accessed.

> Lewis, Sinclair. *Main Street*. New York:
>
> Harcourt, 1920. "The Project Gutenberg
>
> Etext of *Main Street,* by Sinclair Lewis."
>
> Etext#543. May 1996. *Project Gutenberg.*
>
> ftp://src.doc.ic.ac.uk/media/literary/
>
> collections/project_gutenberg/gutenberg/
>
> etext96/mnstr10.txt (14 Dec. 1998).

20. Via Telnet

Give the author of the document you are citing, if known; the title of the object or file in quotation marks; the name of the complete work or site, in italics, if applicable; the name of the maintainer of the site, if applicable; the protocol and complete address, including paths or commands needed to reach the document; and the date of access.

> "The Women's Collection of Electronic Texts."
>
> Maint. Dene Grigar et al. *TWUMOO*. telnet://
>
> 205.165.53.14:8888 A EW WCET
>
> (28 Dec. 1998).

4 Synchronous conference records

21. MOOs, MUDs

MOOs and MUDs function like chat rooms in many ways. Give the name or alias of the author of the message, if known; the type of message or the session title in quotation marks; the title of the site in italics; the protocol and full address, including paths or commands required for access; and the date of the exchange.

> Vanessa. Personal interview. *Mundo Hispanico.*
>
> telnet://moo.syr.edu:8888 (28 Dec. 1998).

22. LANs

To cite a message in a conference created with software such as the InterChange feature of the Daedalus Integrated Writing Environment (DIWE), give the author's name or pseudonym as it appears in the transcript. Always ask the author's permission to quote or cite a message. Identify the software or LAN, as appropriate, and the date. For conference transcripts stored online, give the title and address of the location where the transcript can be found.

> "*Incidents in the Life of a Slave Girl*
>
> InterChange." *DIWE*. University of Texas.
>
> 10 Apr. 1997. *E341L: Women's Popular*
>
> *Culture InterChanges.* http://www.cwrl
>
> .utexas.edu/~women/romance/interchanges/
>
> incidents.html (27 Dec. 1998).

5 Reference tools and databases

23. Entry in Online Dictionary

Give the author's name, if available, or begin with the title of the entry in quotation marks. List the title of the dictionary in italics; give information about previous print publication, if applicable; give the date of publication of the online edition if different from the date of access; and list the electronic address and the date of access.

> Lapiaki, Jolanta A. "Network." *ASL Dictionary*
>
> *Online.* http://dww.deafworldweb.org/
>
> asl/n/network.html (17 Dec. 1998).

No separate publication date is given because the site is updated daily.

24. Article in Online Encyclopedia

Name the author of the article, if available, or begin with the title of the article in quotation marks. After the italicized title of the encyclopedia, give information about the publisher (name and city); list a subscriber service, if applicable; give the copyright date; list the electronic address, including any applicable paths or directories; and give the date accessed.

> Hefner, Alan G. "The Legend of the Buffalo
>
> Dance." *The Encyclopedia Mythica*. M. F.
>
> Lindemans, 1998. http://www.pantheon.org/

```
mythica/articles/1/legend_of_buffalo

dance.html (17 Dec. 1998).
```

25. Information on CD-ROM

List the name of the author or editor, the title of the article or section in quotation marks, the title of the CD-ROM in italics, the version number preceded by *Vers.*, and the city, publisher, and year of publication. Omit the date of access.

```
Rose, Mark, ed. "Elements of Theater." The

    Norton Shakespeare Workshop CD-ROM. Vers.

    1.1. New York: Norton, 1997.
```

26. Article from Online Database

Give the author's name, the title of the article in quotation marks, and the italicized title of the journal or work in which the article originally appeared. List the version or edition number, if applicable; the date of publication; and the page numbers(s) in the original source. Give the name of the database or retrieval service in italics (or the complete electronic address), the file or article number, and the date of access.

```
Wittberg, Patricia. "Deep Structure in

    Community Cultures: The Revival of

    Religious Orders in Roman Catholicism."

    Sociology of Religion. Fall 1997: 239+.

    Searchbank: Expanded Academic ASAP,

    Article #A20245892 (18 Dec. 1998).
```

6 Software
27. Software/Video Game

Give the name of an individual or corporate author; the title of the software or video game in italics; the version number, if applicable; and the place, publisher, and date of publication.

```
Blair, C. Arthur. Black Quest: The Griot.

    Bladensburg, MD: Rediscovery Learning

    Works, 1997.
```

5e Sample COS/humanities-style works cited page

Works Consulted

Brown, Kirk W. *Hazardous Waste and Treatment*.
    Woburn: Butterworth, 1983.

Bugher, Robert D. *Municipal Refuse Disposal*.
    Danville: Interstate, 1970.

Farley, Rose. "Bottom of the Ninth: Permit
Article from   Hearings Begin in TXI's Quest to Become
archive of
an online   the Nation's Largest Toxic Waste
newspaper   Incinerator." *Dallas Observer Online*. 12
    Feb. 1998. *Dallas Observer Archives*.
    http://www.dallasobserver.com/archives/
    1998/021298/news2.html (19 Jan. 1999).

Flack, J. E. *Man and the Quality of His
    Environment*. Boulder: U of Colorado P,
    1967.

Hand, Shane. *Questionnaire on Consumer Habits
    and Attitudes Toward Recycling*.
    Blacksburg, VA, and Upper Marlboro, MD.
    21-25 Feb. 1999.

Hazardous Waste Incineration. New York:
    American Society of Mechanical Engineers,
    1988.

Montague, Peter. "New Study Shows Incinerator
    Ash More Dangerous Than We Realized."
    Rachel's Hazardous Waste News 92 (29 Aug
    1988). http://www.enviroweb.org/pubs/
    rachel/rhwn092.htm (19 Jan. 1999).

Organic Waste Technologies Inc. "Leachate
    Evaporation." 1998. *Corporate author, no individual*
    author or site title

http://www.owtinc.com/leachate_1.htm (19
Jan. 1999).

Pennsylvania Department of Environmental
Protection. "Brownfields Tax Incentive." 1
July 1998. http://www.dep.state.pa.us/
dep/deputate/airwaste/wm/landrecy/Tax/
tax.htm (19 Jan. 1999).

Rathje, William L. "Once and Future Landfills."
National Geographic May 1991: 116-34.

Van Tassel, Alfred J. *Environmental Side
Effects of Rising Industrial Output.*
Lexington, MA: Heath, 1970.

Wiseman, Clark A. "Impediments to Economically
Efficient Solid Waste Management."
Resources 105 (1991): 9-11.

5f Using COS in the sciences (with APA, CBE)

The basic format for citing online sources in a reference list is as follows.

Author's Surname, Initial(s). (Date of document
if different from date of last revision).
Title of document. *Title of complete work
or site* (file or version number). (Edition
or date of last revision). Protocol and
electronic address, access path, or
directories (Date of access).

The author's last name is given first, followed by a comma and the initials of the first and middle names. If no single author is named, use the name of the sponsoring organization, if it appears on the page. If the document date is different from the date of access, place it in parentheses after the author's name, followed by a period and a space. Give the year first, followed by the month, if applicable, in unabbreviated form, and the day. COS/scientific style uses no quotation marks for titles and capitalizes only the first word of a title or subtitle and any proper nouns (except in journal titles, which are capitalized with APA style) follow with a period.

Italicize the title of the complete work or site. List the file, version, or edition number (in parentheses); the date of last revision or modification (in parentheses); the complete electronic address, and the date you accessed the site (in parentheses). For the revision date and date of access, list a numeral for day; an abbreviation for all months except May, June, and July; and the year (for example, *25 June 1942*). Although all of the above information may not apply or be available, provide as much of it as possible in your citation.

```
Brown, M. C. (1997). The past: What has happened
        before. The faces of science: African
        Americans in the sciences (Rev. 31 Aug.
        1998). http://www.lib.lsu.edu/lib/chem/
        display/faces.html#Past (28 Dec. 1998).
```

Guide to COS/Scientific Formats for a Reference List

1. CITATIONS FROM THE WORLD WIDE WEB (WWW)
28. WWW Site
29. WWW Site—Revised, Updated, or Modified
30. WWW Site—Authored by Group, Organization, or Institution
31. WWW Site—Corporate Author
32. WWW Site—Without Named Author, Group, or Title
33. WWW Site—Maintained or Compiled by Individual
34. WWW Site—Government
35. WWW Site—Printed Book Available Online
36. WWW Site—Electronic Book
37. WWW Site—Online Article
38. WWW Site—Article from News Service or Online Newspaper
39. WWW Site—Article from Archive (Previously Published in Print)
40. WWW Site—with Frames
41. WWW Site—Graphic or Audio File

2. EMAIL MESSAGES, DISCUSSION LISTS, OR NEWSGROUPS
42. Email—Personal
43. Email—Discussion List
44. Email—From Newsgroup
45. Email—From Message Archive

3 MATERIALS OBTAINED VIA GOPHER, FTP, OR TELNET
46. Via Gopher or FTP
47. Via Telnet

4. SYNCHRONOUS CONFERENCE RECORDS
48. MOOs, MUDs
49. LANs

5. REFERENCE TOOLS AND DATABASES
50. Entry in Online Dictionary
51. Article in Online Encyclopedia
52. Information on CD-ROM
53. Article from Online Database

6. SOFTWARE
54. Software/Video Game

1 Citations from the World Wide Web (WWW)
28. WWW Site

```
Hochman, W. (1998). Beyond exception: The
    writer's life. The Salt River review, 1
    (1) (Rev. Nov. 1998). http://www.mc
    .maricopa.edu/users/cervantes/SRR/hochman
    .html (20 Dec. 1998).
```

29. WWW Site—Revised, Updated, or Modified

If a date of last revision, updating, or modification is given on the site, indicate it in parentheses immediately after the title, preceded by the abbreviation *Rev.* or *Mod.*

```
AFL-CIO. (1998). Facts about working women.
    Today's unions (Rev. 7 Dec. 1998).
    http://www.aflcio.org/women/wwfacts
    .htm (19 Dec. 1998).
```

30. WWW Site—Authored by Group, Organization, or Institution

If a group, organization, or institution sponsors a site and no individual author is named, use the name of the group in place of an author.

```
International Olympic Committee. Welcome to the
    official site of the International Olympic
    Committee. The official site of the
    International Olympic Committee.
    http://www.olympic.org (27 Dec. 1998).
```

31. WWW Site—Corporate Author

When a corporation serves as the author of a page, use its full name; give the date of publication in parentheses if different from date of access, followed by a period and the page's title.

```
Goodwill Industries International, Inc. (1998).
    Goodwill career links (Rev. 18 Dec. 1998).
    http://www.goodwill.org/about/careerlk
    .htm (19 Dec. 1998).
```

If the complete site has a title different from the name of the corporation used as author, provide it, in italics.

> LatinoLink Enterprises, Inc. (1998). Job bank.
>
>   *LatinoLink*. http://www.latinolink.com/
>
>   joblist.html (29 Dec. 1998).

32. WWW Site—Without Named Author, Group, or Title

When no author or authoring group is named on the Web page, begin with the title of the document, followed by the date of the document (if available), the electronic address, and the date accessed.

> Social statistics briefing room.
>
>   http://www.whitehouse.gov/fsbr/ssbr.html
>
>   (19 Dec. 1998).

If no title is given, begin with file name and type.

> chorusline.mpg [animated graphic file]. http://
>
>   www.juggling.org/animations/chorusline
>
>   .mpg (20 Dec. 1998).

33. WWW Site—Maintained or Compiled by Individual

A maintained site is one in which a Web designer organizes, indexes, and posts information gathered from several sources, often for a sponsoring organization. For a maintained site, give the group or author first, if applicable; the date of publication in parentheses; the title of the site; and, in parentheses; the name of the maintainer followed by the abbreviation *Maint.* For a compiled site that consists primarily of links to other sites, use *Comp.* after the name of the site's creator.

> Southeast Colorado RC&D, Inc. *Colorado Southeast*
>
>   *network*. (A. Bray, Comp.). http://www
>
>   .ruralnet.net/~csn (17 Dec. 1998).

To make specific reference to the work of the maintainer or compiler, place that name first, followed by *Maint.* or *Comp.* in parentheses.

> Freeland, C. (Maint.). (1997, January). *SWIP—The*
>
>   *Society for Women in Philosophy*. http://www
>
>   .uh.edu/~cfreelan/SWIP/ (17 Dec. 1998).

If the maintainer or compiler is not named, simply omit that information.

```
Computers and academic freedom. Academic

    freedom policy statements archive.

    http://www.eff.org/pub/CAF/academic

    (27 Dec. 1998).
```

34. WWW Site—Government

Use the name of the sponsoring government agency in place of the author; then proceed as usual. Note that for a site updated every few minutes, the date of publication is omitted because it is identical with the date of access.

```
U.S. Census Bureau. POPClocks. U.S. Census

    Bureau: The official statistics.

    http://www.census.gov/main/www/popclock.

    html (27 Dec. 1998).
```

35. WWW Site—Printed Book Available Online

An online version of a book first published on paper should be cited with as much original publication information as is available, including the date of publication, the name of the publisher, and the city where the publisher is located. For a book published under a pseudonym, give the real name in brackets. Place the name of the editor of the hypertext version, if you know it, just before the Web address.

```
Twain, M. [S. L. Clemens]. (1869). The

    innocents abroad: Or, the new Pilgrim's

    Progress. Hartford: American.

    http://etext.virginia.edu/railton/innocent/

    iahompag.html (18 Dec. 1998).
```

36. WWW Site—Electronic Book

Electronic "books" vary in type. Some are more accurately described as hypertext narratives or interactive narratives. They may have multiple authors, who may be using pseudonyms and writing synchronously at a MOO or asynchronously, as in the case below. Give the primary author's name, if known; the date of publication in parentheses, if different from the date of last revision; the title of the work in italics; the date of last revision in parentheses; the electronic address; and the date of access.

> *The company therapist.* (1996). (Rev. 19 Dec.
> 1998). http://www.thetherapist.com/
> index.html (21 Dec. 1998).

37. WWW Site—Online Article

List the author(s) and give the date of publication in parentheses,
the article title, and the usual publication information.

> Palmquist, M., Hochman, W., Kolko, B., Golson,
> E., Alexander, J., Barnes, L., & Kiefer, K.
> (1997). Hypertext reflections: Exploring
> the rhetoric, poetics, and pragmatics of
> hypertext. *Kairos, 2*(2). http://english.ttu
> .edu/kairos/2.2/features/reflections/bridge
> .html (16 Dec. 1998).

38. WWW Site—Article from News Service or Online Newspaper

Give the name of the author, if known, or the name of the news
source (for example, *Associated Press*); the title of the article; the title of the
news service or online newspaper in italics; the electronic address; and the
date accessed.

> Espy, D. House votes to impeach Clinton. *Yahoo!*
> *news.* http://dailynews.yahoo.com/
> headlines/ap/washington/story.html?s+v/ap/
> 19981219/pl/ (19 Dec. 1998).

39. WWW Site—Article from Archive (Previously Published in Print)

Give the author's name, the date of publication in parentheses; the
title of the article; the name of the journal and the name of the archive,
both in italics; the address; and the date accessed.

> Hauben, M. F. (1997, February). The Netizens
> and community networks. *Computer mediated*
> *communication magazine, 4*(2). *CMC magazine*
> *archive.* http://www.december.com/cmc/
> mag/1997/feb/hauben.htm (16 Dec. 1998).

40. WWW Site—With Frames

For a document without its own URL, provide the italicized title of the page from which it was linked, then the electronic address of the main page, followed by a single blank space and the link(s) needed to get to the article.

Studies of intermarriage underway. (1995).

Communities in transition, 1(1). http:/

/www.hebrewcollege.edu/wilstein/index.html

Wilstein Institute News (17 Dec. 1998).

41. WWW Site—Graphic or Audio File

Give the name of the artist, photographer, or composer; the date of production; the title of the work (in italics if first published separately); and original publication information. If you wish to refer to the item as part of a Web page, add the title of the page after the title of the file.

Seares, R. (1931, February 26). *Einstein with*

young people. PhotoNet. *California*

Institute of Technology: Institute

archives. http://www.caltech.edu/

cgi-bin/arctohtml?1.8.1-12 (20 Dec. 1998).

2 Email, discussion lists, or newsgroups
42. Email—Personal

Although scientific reference lists seldom include personal email, if you use it, include either the sender's name with the first initial or the log-in name; the date the message was sent, if different from the date of access, in parentheses; and the subject line. In brackets, indicate the kind of message. Always omit personal email addresses and ask the author for permission to use the post.

Osborne. P. Family reunion. [Personal email].

(19 Dec. 1998).

43. Email—Discussion List

Provide the sender's real name or log-in name; the date the message was sent in parentheses; the subject line as the title; the name of the discussion list in italics; and the address of the list. Then give the name of the discussion list, its address, and the date of access.

```
Kemp, F. Digital learning communities. RHETNET.
    RHETNET-L@MIZZOU1.missouri.edu (4 Sep.
    1996).
```

44. Email—From Newsgroup

List the author's name or alias; the date the message was posted if other than the date of access; the subject line; the name of the newsgroup, if applicable, in italics; the protocol and address; and the date accessed.

```
Maffetone, P. (1998, December 13). Re: Running
    and carbohydrate diet. news:rec.running.
    (22 Mar. 1999).
```

45. Email—From Message Archive

Give the author's real name or log-in name; the date of posting in parentheses, if different from the date of access; the subject line of the message; the name of the discussion list in italics; and the list address. Then give the name of the archive in italics, the archive address of the post, and the date of access.

```
Caraveo, S. (1998, August 20). New stuff at
    nativeWeb. News, announcements, and
    information list. nw-news@nativeWeb.org.
    Wotanging Ikche: Native American news
    archives. http://www.nativeWeb.org/
    archives/news/9808/msg00000.html
    (21 Dec. 1998).
```

3 Materials obtained via gopher, ftp, or telnet
46. Via Gopher or FTP

Give the author's name; the date of original publication, if applicable, in parentheses; the title of the work (with book titles in italics); and, if previously published in print, the city and publisher. Give the title of the electronic version if it has been altered from the original; the file or version numbers, if applicable; the date of electronic publication or last revision in parentheses; the title of the database, if applicable, in italics; and the gopher or ftp protocol and address, paths or directories, and date accessed.

```
Lewis, S. (1920). Main Street. New York:
     Harcourt. The Project Gutenberg etext of
     Main street, by Sinclair Lewis.
     (Etext#543). (May 1996). Project
     Gutenberg. ftp://src.doc.ic.ac.uk/media/
     literary/collections/project_gutenberg/
     gutenberg/etext96/mnstr10.txt (14 Dec.
     1998).
```

47. Via Telnet

Give the author of the document you are citing, if known; the date of publication (in parentheses) if known and different from the date of access; the title of the work or object cited; the name of the complete work or site, in italics, if applicable; the date of publication, if known; the protocol and complete telnet address, followed by a single blank space and a list of any directories or commands needed to access the work; and the date of access.

```
The women's collection of electronic texts. (D.
     Grigar et al., Maint.). TWUMOO. telnet:/
     /205.165.53.14:8888 A EW WCET (28 Dec.
     1998).
```

4 Synchronous conference records

48. MOOs, MUDs

Give the name or alias of the author of the message, if known; the type of message or title of the session; the italicized title of the MOO or MUD site, if applicable; the protocol and complete address, including paths and any commands needed to access it; and the date of the exchange.

```
Vanessa. Personal interview. Mundo Hispanico.
     telnet://moo.syr.edu:8888 (28 Dec. 1998).
```

49. LANs

To cite a message in a conference created with software such as Daedalus InterChange, give the author's name or pseudonym as it appears in the transcript, the date of the session, and its title. Identify the software or LAN, as appropriate, and give the date. For transcripts stored online, give the title and address of the location where the transcript can be found. Always request the author's permission to quote an InterChange message.

> *Incidents in the life of a slave girl.*
> InterChange. (1997, April 10). *DIWE.*
> University of Texas. *E341L: Women's*
> *Popular Culture InterChanges.* http://www
> .cwrl.utexas.edu/~women/romance/
> interchanges/incidents.html (27 Dec. 1998).

5 Reference tools and databases

50. Entry in Online Dictionary

Give the author's name, if available, and the date of publication if different from the date of access; or begin with the entry as the title, followed by the date of publication. List the title of the dictionary in italics, and give information about previous publication, if applicable; give the electronic address and the date of access.

> Lapiaki, J. A. Network. *ASL dictionary online.*
> http://dww.deafworldWeb.org/asl
> (17 Dec. 1998).

No separate publication date is given because the dictionary is modified daily.

51. Article in Online Encyclopedia

Name the author of the article, if available, followed by the date of the document. If no author is named, begin with the title of the article, followed by the date. Give the title of the encyclopedia in italics; list the name of the publisher and information about print publication, if applicable; list the subscriber service, if applicable; give the electronic address, including paths or directories needed to reach the document; and add the date accessed.

> Hefner, A. G. (1998). The legend of the buffalo
> dance. *The encyclopedia mythica.* M. F.
> Lindemans. http://www.pantheon.org/
> mythica/articles/l/legend_of_buffalo_dance
> .html (17 Dec. 1998).

52. Information on CD-ROM

Give author's or editor's surname and initial(s), followed by *Ed.* in parentheses, if applicable. List the year of publication in parentheses, the title of the article or section of the disk cited, and the title of the disk in italics. Give the version number, preceded by the word *Version* in parentheses and followed by the publisher's city and name.

Rose, M. (Ed.). (1997). Elements of theater.

The Norton Shakespeare workshop (Version

1.1). New York: Norton.

53. Article from Online Database

Give the author's surname and initial(s); the date of publication in parentheses; the title of the article; original publication information, including the title of the publication; volume and file numbers, if applicable, in parentheses; the name of the database in italics; the article or file number in parentheses (or the complete electronic address); and the date of access.

Wittberg, P. (1997, Fall). Deep structure in

community cultures: The revival of

religious orders in Roman Catholicism.

Sociology of religion. 239+. *Searchbank:*

Expanded academic ASAP, Article #A20245892

(12 Dec. 1998).

6 Software
54. Software/Video Game

Blair, C. Arthur. (1997). *Black quest: The*

griot. Bladensburg, MD: Rediscovery

Learning Works.

5g Sample COS Reference List

References

Coyle, E. F., Coggan, A. R., Hopper, M. K., &

Walters, T. J. (1988). Determinants of

endurance in well-trained cyclists.
Journal of Applied Physiology, 64, 2622-
2630.

David, C., & Cowles, M. (1991). Body image and
exercise. *Sex Roles, 25,* 33-34.

Drewnowski, A., & Yee, D. K. (1987). Men and
body image: Are males satisfied with their
body weight? *Psychosomatic Medicine, 49,*
626-634.

Interbike 1992 directory. (1992). Costa Mesa,
CA: Primedia.

Matheny, F. (1986, February 5). Solo cycling.
Volo News, 157.

Meyer, J. (1994, Winter). Alison Sydor,
cyclist, on equity in cycling. *Action.*
http://www.makeithappen.com/wis/readings/
insydor.htm (9 Nov. 1998).

Schneider, D., & Greenberg, M. (1992). Choice
of exercise: A predictor of behavioral
risks. *Research Quarterly for Exercise and
Sport, 9,* 231-245.

Worthington, R. G. (1998). *Labor power racing:
lung busters, leg breakers.*
http://www.mesothel.com/pages/labpower.htm
(9 Nov. 1998).

Zimberoff, B. F. (1996). Ocean to ocean on two
wheels: Harassment on the road. *Armchair
World NetEscapes.*
http://www.armchair.com/escape/bike7.html
(9 Nov. 1998).

*An article
previously
published in
a periodical*

*Citation for
a Web site*